D1541407

Ghana

Rachel Naylor

Oxfam

First published by Oxfam GB in 2000

© Oxfam GB 2000

ISBN 0 85598 431 7

A catalogue record for this publication is available from the British Library.

All rights reserved. Reproduction, copy, transmission, or translation of any part of this publication may be made only under the following conditions:

- With the prior written permission of the publisher; or
- With a licence from the Copyright Licensing Agency Ltd., 90 Tottenham Court Road, London W1P 9HE, UK, or from another national licensing agency; or
- For quotation in a review of the work; or
- Under the terms set out below.

This publication is copyright, but may be reproduced by any method without fee for teaching purposes, but not for resale. Formal permission is required for all such uses, but normally will be granted immediately. For copying in any other circumstances, or for re-use in other publications, or for translation or adaptation, prior written permission must be obtained from the publisher, and a fee may be payable.

Available from the following agents:

USA: Stylus Publishing LLC,
  PO Box 605, Herndon, VA 20172-0605, USA
  tel: +1 (0)703 661 1581; fax: + 1(0)703 661 1547;
  email: styluspub@aol.com; website www.styluspub.com

Canada: Fernwood Books Ltd,
  PO Box 9409, Stn. 'A', Halifax, N.S. B3K 5S3, Canada
  tel: +1 (0)902 422 3302; fax: +1 (0)902 422 3179;
  e-mail: fernwood@istar.ca

India: Maya Publishers Pvt Ltd,
  113-B, Shapur Jat, New Delhi-110049, India
  tel: +91 (0)11 649 4850; fax: +91 (0)11 649 1039;
  email: surit@del2.vsnl.net.in

  K Krishnamurthy,
  23 Thanikachalan Road, Madras 600017, India
  tel: +91 (0)44 434 4519; fax: +91 (0)44 434 2009;
  email: ksm@md2.vsnl.net.in

South Africa, Zimbabwe, Botswana, Lesotho, Namibia, Swaziland:
  David Philip Publishers,
  PO Box 23408, Claremont 7735, South Africa
  tel: +27 (0)21 64 4136; fax: +27(0)21 64 3358;
  email: dppsales@iafrica.com

Tanzania: Mkuki na Nyota Publishers,
  PO Box 4246, Dar es Salaam, Tanzania
  tel/fax: +255 (0)51 180479, email: mkuki@ud.co.tz

Australia: Bush Books,
  PO Box 1958, Gosford, NSW 2250, Australia
  tel: +61 (0)2 043 233 274; fax: +61 (0)2 092 122 468,
  email: bushbook@ozemail.com.au

Rest of the world: contact Oxfam Publishing,
  274 Banbury Road, Oxford OX2 7DZ, UK.
  tel. +44 (0)1865 311 311; fax +44 (0)1865 313 925;
  email publish@oxfam.org.uk;
  website www.oxfam.org.uk/publications.html

Printed by
Information Press, Southfield Road, Eynsham OX8 1JJ, UK

Published by
Oxfam GB, 274 Banbury Road, Oxford OX2 7DZ, UK

Series designed by
Richard Morris, Stonesfield Design.
This title designed by Richard Morris.
Typeset in FF Scala and Gill Sans.

Cover designed by
Rowie Christopher

Oxfam GB is a registered charity, no. 202 918, and is a member of Oxfam International.

Photo acknowledgements:

Toby Adamson (©Oxfam GB): 5 main, 7 main, 9 bottom, 10 top, 12, 14 left, 21, 32, 33, 35 bottom, 38, 40 right, 43, 44, 46, 47, 48, 49, 54, 55, 56, 58, 60, 61, 62 main, 63, 65, 70, 72, 73, 77, 78, 79, 81, 86

Sarah Errington (©Oxfam GB): 5 top, 6 right, 7 top, 9 top, 10 bottom left, 24, 35 top, 41, 42/3 main, 45, 51, 74 left

Rachel Naylor (©Oxfam GB): 71

Marcus Rose (©Oxfam GB): 6 left, 20, 25, 30 main, 53, 64

Penny Tweedie (©Oxfam GB): 4, 10 bottom right, 13, 15, 26, 28, 39, 40 left, 52, 62 bottom, 66, 67, 69, 74 right, 85

AKG: 14 main, 17, 80

British Museum: 59, 68

Ghanaian High Commission London: 31

Hulton Getty: 19, 23

Ike Essel, *Uhuru*: 27

Tanko: 36

Contents

Selling fish on the quay in Elmina, situated on the Gulf of Guinea. The Portuguese, who were among the first Europeans to reach West Africa, built Elmina Castle in 1481.

Introduction: all in a nation

▲ Women in Zawara village, northwest Ghana, draw water from a hand-operated well that has relieved the women of long treks to find water.

To paint a picture of Ghana requires a palette of many colours. On the Gulf of Guinea, fishermen haul their canoes onto palm-fringed white beaches. Amid towering tropical rainforests, women with babies on their backs walk tall, headloading firewood. In the north, fat baobab trees dominate wide expanses of dry savannah where farmers bend double, weeding groundnut crops. Hauntingly beautiful white-washed castles overlook the coast, stainless walls masking a sordid past; there are low-rise, rusty zinc-roofed cities and tiny thatch-roofed villages. Throbbing notes of the latest highlife and gospel tunes contrast with the midnight melancholy sounds of Fulani pipers' flutes. At stations, anxious calls of 'ice water' come from young girls hawking refreshments in torn t-shirts. The horns of impatient *trotro* drivers mingle with the regular thump of sweating cooks pounding yams for weary travellers. Acrid smoke spills from Tema's workshops. The smell of boiling *light soup* stings the air with pepper. Sharp-suited officials inhabit Accra offices, and on the city's catwalks, beautiful men and women sport wax-print body creations. Rich black and red robes worn by solemn Akan mourners vie with vibrant many-coloured cloth strips slung from the looms of Kente weavers.

► Markets like this one in Kumasi, Ghana's second largest city, offer a wide choice of fabrics to fashion-conscious shoppers.

▲ A land of contrasts: Nima, a crowded neighbourhood on the outskirts of Accra, and a grain store in a rural village in northern Ghana.

In the contemporary world, Ghana is renowned for its cocoa and its gold, and for being the birthplace of UN Secretary General Kofi Annan. What else is behind this picture?

Named after a wealthy and powerful mediaeval empire, Ghana is both a nation and a collection of disparate peoples. Ghanaians have a strong sense of national identity and are proud of their history and their independence. As citizens of the 'Black Star of Africa', they unite behind their football teams: the Black Meteors, the Black Satellites, the Black Stars, and, not forgetting the women's national team, the Black Queens. Ghana-wide, there are shared cultural traditions, including the proverbial Ghanaian hospitality.

At the same time, Ghanaians are divided into about 60 distinct ethnic groups with their own traditions, languages, ambitions, and grievances. There are four main groups: Akan speakers (mainly living in the Brong-Ahafo, Ashanti, Western, Central, and Eastern regions), the Ga-Adangbe (Greater Accra region), Mole-Dagbani speakers (Upper West, Upper East, and the Northern regions) and the Ewe (Volta region). There are also significant ethnic minorities in Ghana, such as the Lebanese, who dominate in medium-scale business, and the Fulani, many of whom are cattle keepers by tradition, who live in many parts of West Africa.

Since Ghana's borders are a product of colonialism rather than following ethnic lines, many Ghanaians have ethnic and kinship connections with neighbouring countries. The Ewe and Konkomba people span the border to Togo in the east, Akan speakers live on both sides of the western frontier with Côte d'Ivoire, and the Frafra and Mossi live across the northern border in Burkina Faso.

Ethnic identities evolve with political and economic conditions and vary according to the standpoint of the commentator – but we can sketch a broad outline. The biggest ethnic family in Ghana is Akan-speaking and includes subjects of the centralised Ashanti, Brong, and Fanti traditional states. Akan peoples are culturally distinctive in Ghana because they have a tradition of inheritance through the maternal line. The Ewe have a less centralised form of traditional political rule, and unlike Akan, the Ewe language group is made up of dialects not all of which are mutually intelligible. The Ewe claim to be the inventors of the famous *kente* cloth, worn like togas by men and as wrap-arounds by women, whose colourful patterns carry great cultural significance. Ga people were well known in Ghana for a unique residence tradition whereby husbands and wives lived separately with their own kin. Today, they are highly urbanised, living in Accra, the national capital.

▼ *Nakori mosque near Wa, built in Malian style with white-washed mud walls and black-painted wooden supports. The thick walls keep the interior very cool.*

In the savannah environment of the north live the citizens of Gonja, Dagomba, Mamprusi, and other smaller states, and peoples which have traditionally lived in non-centralised societies, for example the Tallensi, Konkomba, Dagarti, Frafra, Bimoba, Bulsa, and Sisaala. Northern Ghanaians have distinct social and cultural traditions. The cultural association of northern chiefs with horses can easily be spotted, as can the traditional smock dress worn by men from many of the ethnic groups. Linguistics experts note that while Akan, Ewe and Ga have a common ancestral language (which they term Kwa), most northern languages have a common parent language (Gur) which is only very remotely related to Kwa.

A north-south divide, which follows this cultural and environmental difference, is an important watershed in Ghanaian life. It is reinforced by different experiences of history: in the colonial era, economic and social development were promoted in the south whereas the north was largely administered as a labour reserve. To some extent, the focus of government development work remains in the south. As a result, poverty and underdevelopment are concentrated in the north, although there are pockets of deep disadvantage in many parts of Ghana. The north also has a different religious

▲ Men cycling home after drumming at a funeral in Tampion village in the Northern Region.

and political history. This area saw an early Islamic influence while later Christian missionary activity was curtailed here under colonialism. The unique dynamic of the relationship between the centralised traditional states and the non-centralised ethnic groups of the northern area was, and remains, central to its local political history.

There are also stark contrasts between rich and poor in Ghana, but by international standards the disparities are moderate. Ghanaians tend to maintain links with large extended families – ties of affection, but also links which entail obligations and benefits and act as lines of redistribution of wealth and opportunity.

The majority of Ghanaians continue to live on the land, and there is a strong contrast between urban and rural life. But again, there are solid links between the two in Ghana, because of family relationships and economic necessity. In all but the largest cities, families travel to surrounding areas to farm in order to supplement urban earnings. Wealthier city Ghanaians may not visit the village each weekend, but usually invest capital in cash cropping and make time to visit their plantations during the agricultural year. The links between city and village are only broken if the urban dweller cannot afford to meet obligations in his or her home village, especially helping with expensive funeral rites.

Since the mid-1980s, international financial institutions have hailed Ghana as a flagship for economic reform in Africa. Despite the plaudits, for people like Kofi Poku-Agyemang, Ghana seems to have been ravaged by economic and political problems. Has the country that had such bright prospects when it became the first sub-Saharan African nation to gain its independence from colonial rule failed to fulfil its promise?

This book tries to answer this question by introducing some of the main obstacles to prosperity and democracy in Ghana today and showing how ordinary people experience, and struggle to cope with, these realities. It looks at the impact of the country's troubled history, of the ongoing attempts to put Ghana's economic and political house in order, as well as the conflict which has flared up in recent years. The book ends by asking what hope there is for the future.

WORKING IN THE CITY, FARMING IN THE COUNTRY

Kofi Poku-Agyemang is typical of the new generation of young urban Ghanaians. His family considered education a priority: Kofi and his brother and sister were sent to school and studied hard. But opportunities are still limited, and Kofi now runs a communication centre in Kumasi where people come to make telephone calls. Kofi manages to make a slim profit but it is not enough to meet his family's needs. He lives with his father, a retired teacher whose small pension cannot make up the shortfall. Like many Ghanaians, the Poku-Agyemangs go to their farm every few weeks. They cultivate maize, yams, and cocoa which they sell to boost their income. They keep some of the yams for family consumption.

Tropical coast to sub-Sahara

▲ ▼ *Northern Ghana in the dry and rainy season: from dry red earth to fertile green landscape.*

Ghana lies on the coast of West Africa, on the Gulf of Guinea. It is bordered by Burkina Faso to the north, Togo to the east, and Côte d'Ivoire to the west. The dry savannah grasslands of interior West Africa cover northern Ghana, with low and unpredictable rainfall concentrated in a single rainy season between April and October. The area has poor soils affected by bush fires, erosion, and desertification; problems which worsen the further north you travel. Further south, the vegetation becomes more lush. In the rainforest belt of central and southern Ghana, logging has depleted much of the tree cover but the soils remain fertile. The rains here are moderate and more predictable, falling in two seasons which permits double cropping. The southern coastal strip is mostly dry grassland.

The dominant geographical feature in Ghana is the Volta Lake, enlarged in the 1960s by the construction of the Akosombo dam to become the world's largest artificial lake. As well as providing an economic livelihood for fishing communities, it is also navigable, and there is constant north-south passenger and freight traffic. The Volta even boasts a hospital boat which takes medical services to remote communities on the

▲ Gambaga escarpment near Nakpanduri, during the rainy season.

▼ A building in Bonwire, near Kumasi, bears witness to the colonial influence on Ghana, and the futuristic National Theatre in Accra dominates the city's skyline.

lake. Ghana is also served by a rapidly improving road network: reliable public transport connects small towns, cities, and international destinations.

The most dramatic land feature is the Gambaga escarpment which rises 457m over the hot plains of northernmost Ghana. The Akwapim hills near Accra provide a cool, lush respite from the sun-baked coastal cities.

Scattered around Ghana are forest and nature reserves. Some preserve rainforest while other conserve wildlife, including populations of savannah elephants, lions, and antelope. Some of the reserves, such as Kakum National Park in the Central Region or Mole Game Reserve in the Northern Region, are geared up for safari tours, hosting local and international visitors.

Ghanaian cities are mainly low-rise and are divided into areas named after the villages which they swallowed up in their expansion: in the capital, the term 'Accra' denotes a small area which used to be a Ga village. The exception to this rule is Tema, a new port which was planned on a grid matrix and is divided into numbered Communities, each with its own market and post office.

But perhaps the most dramatic buildings in Ghana are the oldest. A series of coastal forts which were used for the slave trade dominate the shoreline from east to west and are currently in use as museums, prisons, and hotels. In the north, striking black-and-white half-timbered mosques and the Wa palace stand out against the dry-season skyline. Nakori mosque is one of the oldest, reputedly dating from the seventeenth century and still in use.

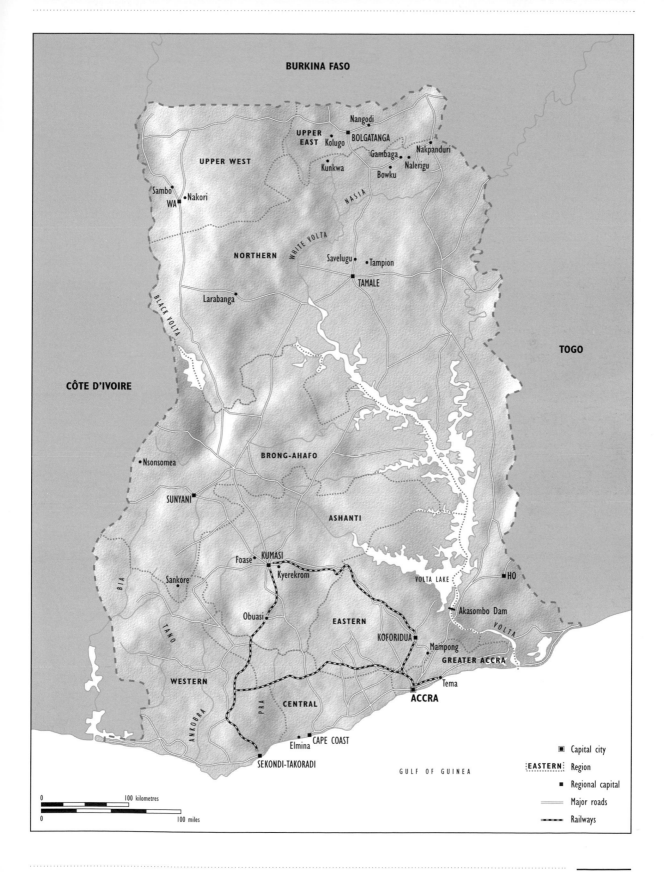

BURKINA FASO

Nangodi

UPPER
EAST

Kolugo BOLGATANGA

Nakpanduri

Gambaga

UPPER WEST

Kunkwa

Nalerigu

Bowku

Sambo

Nakori

WA

NASIA

NORTHERN

WHITE VOLTA

Savelugu

Tampion

TAMALE

CÔTE D'IVOIRE

TOGO

BLACK VOLTA

Larabanga

Nsonsomea

BRONG-AHAFO

SUNYANI

ASHANTI

Foase KUMASI

VOLTA LAKE

HO

Kyerekrom

BIA

Sankore

Obuasi

EASTERN

Akasombo Dam

VOLTA

KOFORIDUA

TANO

Mampong

GREATER ACCRA

WESTERN

PRA

CENTRAL

ACCRA Tema

ANKOBRA

Elmina CAPE COAST

SEKONDI-TAKORADI

GULF OF GUINEA

■ Capital city

EASTERN Region

■ Regional capital

Major roads

Railways

0   100 kilometres

0   100 miles

From Gold Coast to Ghana

The earliest archaeological remains of human activity in Ghana date from approximately 10,000 BC. But most peoples found in Ghana today are the descendants of more recent immigrants, who came from the north and east and had established states by the end of the sixteenth century AD. Some peoples established non-state 'segmentary' societies without secular leaders, but even their histories were strongly influenced by the development of the states.

The rise of the states was associated with the growth of trade in gold and slaves between West and northern Africa across the Sahara desert. States attempted to control and tax this trade. The most well-known state, the Ashanti empire, located in the forest area of central Ghana, began as a small kingdom centred on its capital Kumasi. The Ashanti earned great wealth through monopolisation of gold mining and trade, and expanded through treaty and conquest to control much of what is present-day Ghana. The most important symbol of the state remains the golden stool, equivalent of a throne, known as the 'soul' of Ashanti.

In the savannah areas, the Mamprusi, Dagomba, and Nanumba states trace common ancestry to an immigrant group. They monopolised the horse as a means of warfare. (The horse could not be used in the forest areas, where the tsetse fly, which spreads the fatal disease trypanosomasis to horses and cattle, is endemic.) The horse remains an important symbol of chiefship in the north. The gun was the most important means of subjugation in the southern states.

These northern states were strongly influenced by Islam, brought along the trade routes from Islamic states elsewhere in the savannah. With Islam also came writing.

◄ A statue in Kumasi which represents the conjuring of the golden stool from the sky. According to legend, Okomfo Anokye, priest to the great Ashanti king Osei Tutu I, performed this feat in the late seventeenth century. When British colonists wanted to take the stool away as a sign of victory, the Ashanti handed over a replica.

► A symbol of chiefly status depicted on a compound wall at the National Cultural Centre in Tamale.

▲ *Cape Coast castle, headquarters of British operations from 1665 to 1876, where thousands of slaves were held in dungeons before being transported across the Atlantic.*

ANCIENT GHANA

'Ghana' was a fabulously wealthy and powerful early West African state whose prosperity was built on its control of the gold trade. It was situated to the north west of present-day Ghana. Although it went into decline in the eleventh century, its fame lives on. Because of its reputation and its foundation in gold, 'Ghana' was chosen as the name of the former 'Gold Coast' when the country won its independence from British rule in 1957.

The relationship with new European arrivals

The lure of gold and slaves brought European traders to the coast of Africa as soon as sailing technology permitted. The interaction of the African states and the new arrivals was to have a profound influence on the area that is now Ghana. Africans' drive to profit from the new trading opportunities afforded by the arrival of European traders accelerated state formation. While Ga and Fante peoples organised themselves to control opportunities for gain as 'middlemen' on the coast, interior states crystallised around control of the gold trade (the Akan states) and later the slave trade (the Ashanti, Fante and Ahanta, and northern states). At the same time, slavery took a huge toll on the populations of the interior.

The first traders to arrive were French; by the end of the fourteenth century they had set up a trading post at Elmina. Although they abandoned it, the Portuguese later established themselves in the same place, building the first coastal fort at Elmina in the late fifteenth century. Another century on, Danish and Swedish traders started to establish themselves, and the British soon followed suit. The Europeans constructed forts for defence against African land attack and sea attack by other Europeans. Because of their initial interest in the gold trade, the stretch of coast along which their castles were built became known as the 'Gold Coast'.

The rising demand for labour from the plantations established in the Americas during the sixteenth century resulted in the trans-Atlantic slave trade becoming more important than gold. This foul trade saw slaves kept in the most intolerable, filthy, overcrowded conditions in the coastal forts and then on board slave ships. Death rates were extremely high. It is estimated that 6.3 million slaves were shipped from West Africa to the Americas in total, about 4.5 million between 1701 and 1810.

Trading patterns continued to influence state development in Ghana, as states competed with each other to benefit from the new trading opportunities. They traded slaves for guns, textiles, and other imported items. Some coastal peoples established protection agreements with the Europeans to defend themselves against Ashanti incursions from the

'The Golden Coast, so called by Europeans on account of its abundant and copious yield of gold, ... the mother not only of many good things and treasures of nature but also of the most successful minds.'

Professor Gothelf Loescher, University of Wittenberg, Germany, at the PhD award ceremony for Dr Anthony William Amo, first-known Ghanaian to be awarded a doctorate in 1734.

▲ *European missionaries also brought their architectural styles: St Peter's Cathedral in Kumasi.*

▶ *This German etching from 1684 illustrates the colonisers' representation of Africans which emphasises the superiority of Europeans, by implication denying the existence of highly developed African cultures and political structures.*

interior. States in the interior sold slaves captured in war and perhaps also in slave-raiding campaigns, in an extension of the early trans-Saharan slave-trade. Slaves were also a part of the social structure of the states themselves, although they may have been treated better there than in the new European trade. The trans-Atlantic slave trade led to a depopulation of the sub-continent, particularly of young men. Although the area was sparsely populated, it is estimated that during the peak of the trade about 5,000 slaves were transported every year from the Gold Coast alone.

During the seventeenth century, Christian missionaries began to arrive from Europe. Their interactions with Africans also had a strong influence on the development of Ghana: as well as preaching and church-building, the missionaries built schools and agricultural stations. The first European-style school in Ghana had been established by the Portuguese at Elmina castle in the fifteenth century. Koranic schools were set up later, probably in the seventeenth century. The first Ghanaian headmaster – Philip Quaque, of the Castle School in Cape Coast, who died in 1816 – is still honoured annually.

Missionary conversion, and agricultural and educational activities were largely confined to the south of the country, and this headstart, especially in education, has had an important influence on the regional disparities in development in Ghana.

There were many intermarriages between coastal African families and Europeans, whose children, although dismissed as 'mulattos' and often looked down upon by other Africans and Europeans, had the chance to gain an education. Some of them went on to create successful trading dynasties and to become scholars of distinction. Surnames still common in Cape Coast attest to these relationships, such as Brew, Quist, Mills and de Graft.

► *A mural of Tetteh Quarshie among cocoa trees. Often, plantain trees are planted alongside cocoa plantations, and their leaves used in fermenting the cocoa beans.*

The advent of cocoa

Tetteh Quarshie, a Ghanaian, first brought cocoa to Ghana in 1878, heralding an economic revolution developed wholly by Ghanaians. The crop was quickly taken up by small-scale farmers who sold to buyers for export to European markets. As the sector developed, labour demands led to the migration of men from the poorer north to work on the cocoa plantations. This set up patterns of seasonal and long-term migration which are still evident today. Ghana remains among the leading producers of cocoa – one of the world's favourite crops.

British consolidation of power

By the nineteenth century, Britain was the most important European power on the Gold Coast. Through treaties and conquest it established the Gold Coast Colony in 1876, the Ashanti Protectorate in 1886, and the Northern Territories' Protectorate in 1902. German Togoland became a League of Nations Mandate after the First World War and was administered with the Gold Coast until 1956, when residents voted to merge with the Gold Coast.

British rule was authoritarian and exploitative. It aimed at the extraction of revenue from the colony, achieved by taxing gold exports and the emerging cocoa industry. The Colony and Protectorates were administered through local chiefs under Britain's policy of 'indirect rule'. In the segmentary societies, which had no traditional chiefs, these positions were created artificially. In some cases, indirect rule bolstered the power of traditional chiefs; in others, where unpopular new chiefs were created or existing chiefs were assisted to rule over segmentary peoples, it gave rise to opposition.

Yet it was through indirect rule that traditions of Western-style local democracy and administration were established, and at the national level, a democratic tradition slowly developed through the limited involvement of Africans in the colony's Legislative Council. Legislative and Executive Councils were set up in 1850 to assist Governors with their work, in a purely advisory role. The Executive Council made recommendations on legislation and tax and consisted of a small body of British officials. The Legislative Council included the Executive council and other unofficial members, all appointed by the British government and initially chosen from British merchant interests. It was not until the turn of the twentieth century that Africans became Council members. The first six African members included three chiefs; all six came from Accra, Cape Coast and Sekondi, so they were hardly representative of the colony and protectorates.

In 1925, an element of democracy was introduced when Governor Guggisberg created provincial councils of chiefs in all areas except the Northern Territories. Each council was permitted to elect six chiefs as unofficial members of the Legislative Council. Even so, this was really a move to protect British interests rather than to promote democracy. By limiting nominations to the Legislative Council to chiefs, educated Africans were left out in the cold, and a divide was created between the chiefs and the educated people.

Governor Guggisberg also put in place some development schemes as part of a ten-year plan to promote the export trade and administration of the colony. However, most of these development benefits accrued to the south. Forced labour from the north was recruited to work on many of the southern projects, increasing male depopulation of the north that had been triggered by the growth of cocoa farming. Deep-water harbours at Tema and Takoradi, a railway system linking southern commercial and mining centres, and roads were constructed. Agricultural projects were set up, mainly to assist cocoa production in the south. An education system was established to train African personnel for the administration, but again mainly benefited students from the south.

The struggle for independence

Prior to the nineteenth century the British government had no direct dealings with the Gold Coast. Rather, private companies such as the Royal Africa Company (which later merged with other venture to became the British Africa Company of Merchants) looked after Britain's trade interests. When the slave trade was abolished, the British government faced the question of whether to continue ties with the Gold Coast, as the abolitionists urged. The government decided to proceed with the drive towards political control of the Gold Coast for two main reasons. The first was to protect British trading interests which were threatened by a series of Ashanti invasions of the coastal area between 1807 and 1814. The second reason was ideological: a tide of imperialism was sweeping Europe, and Britain did not want to be left behind.

Africans were involved in spearheading the anti-slavery campaign in Europe. Ottobah Cugoano, a Fante man, published 'Thoughts and Sentiments on Slavery' in England in 1797, marshalling humanitarian and economic arguments against slavery. Cugoano had made his way from slavery in the West Indies to freedom.

Crown government over the coastal forts was established in 1821, later relinquished to the British Africa Company of Merchants, and reinstated in 1843, providing protection and wielding authority over several coastal ethnic groups. From then on, British rule was extended through treaty and conquest. As a tax regime was introduced, economic exploitation became systematised. Revenue-raising began in 1852 in an agreement between the Governor and chiefs under British protection.

As Britain's exploitative imperial rule in the Gold Coast took hold, so a shared sense of patriotism began to evolve among the formerly divided Africans. Struggles over land were the first arena in which their ambitions were played out. After King Aggrey of Cape Coast was exiled by the British because he refused to cede land to them in the nineteenth century, an early nationalist movement was formed. The new education system bred an elite class who began to agitate for African rights. In 1896, members of this elite formed the Aboriginal Rights' Protection Society, again to protest against threats to traditional land tenure.

By the 1920s, the struggle had moved to a demand for elected representation on the Gold Coast Colony's Legislative Council. John Mensah Sarbah, a lawyer, was one of the movement's leaders. Although partial representation was granted in 1925, it was not until 1946 that elected members formed a decisive majority on the Council and African representatives from the Ashanti Protectorate were included.

Before the Second World War, the nationalist struggle was mainly confined to the educated class. Dr J. B. Danquah, also a lawyer, and others encouraged the formation of youth movements which became the fore-runners of the popular struggle. But during the war, ordinary African soldiers were recruited to fight alongside their British counterparts, mostly in Burma. Their experiences of fighting had a profound impact on African

▼ *The Prince of Wales (later King Edward VIII) meets Ashanti chiefs (many of them wearing kente) in the 1920s. The umbrella signifies chiefly authority.*

servicemen, yet after the war they were expected to resume dependant and subservient positions, with little or no compensation for their contribution. The resentment this caused led to the Ghanaian nationalist movement becoming nation-wide.

In 1947, the United Gold Coast Convention (UGCC) was formed, the first nationalist movement which had self-government as its goal. Its founders were called 'the Big Six': Dr J.B. Danquah, Mr Obetsibi-Lamptey, Edward Akuffo-Addo, Ako Adjei, William Ofori Atta, and Dr Kwame Nkrumah. Nkrumah had been invited from London, where he was studying law, to be the UGCC's general secretary. He was arrested for activism, and later broke with the Convention, which aimed for independence only in the shortest possible time. Nkrumah, a charismatic speaker, formed the more radical Convention Peoples' Party (CPP), which demanded immediate self-government, and soon developed a mass following. He and his followers became known as the 'verandah boys', because they slept anywhere when campaigning, a symbol of their identification with the people.

▲ *The Big Six: members of the nationalist elite Nkrumah, Obetsebi-Lamptey, Adjei, Akuffo-Addo, Danquah, and Ofori Atta.*

The issue of the treatment of African ex-servicemen again altered the course of history in 1948: a peaceful march, organised to demand a resettlement package promised to ex-servicemen, was making its way to the colonial seat of government at Osu Castle in Accra when it was stopped at a police barricade. The British Commanding Officer at the barrier ordered his men to shoot at the marchers. When the African second-in-command countermanded the order and the police did not fire, the Commanding Officer shot into the crowd himself, killing three ex-servicemen. Their deaths sparked rioting in Accra and other cities and further strengthened the numbers and the resolve of the independence movement. The three men killed are still commemorated at Ghana's annual independence celebrations.

The CPP won the elections for a new Legislative Assembly in 1951. Nkrumah gained a seat despite being in prison for instigating 'positive action', strikes, and non-violent resistance. As imprisonment had given Nkrumah martyr status, the British had no choice but to release Nkrumah and invite him to form a government.

For another five years, control over defence and foreign policy remained in the hands of the British. In 1956, the CPP under Nkrumah as Prime Minister passed a motion calling for independence, which was quickly approved by the British parliament. Renamed Ghana, the country gained its independence on 6 March 1957, the first independent nation in sub-Saharan Africa.

From dream to despair

From popular independence leader to one-party ruler: Kwame Nkrumah attending the 1965 Commonwealth conference in London.

At independence, Ghana started out with substantial sums in the national accounts and a flourishing economy based on cocoa and mineral exports. Nkrumah's vision was of an industrialised, 'modern' Ghana, to be achieved by putting in place his own brand of socialism, with state-sponsored industrialisation and government-led mechanisation of agriculture. National savings and taxes on the cocoa and mineral sectors were to fund the new investment.

In keeping with this vision, Nkrumah nationalised foreign-owned businesses and started the construction of factories from tomato-canning to sugar-refining. Capital-intensive agriculture projects were initiated, such as rice farming with tractors. Collective farms based on socialist principles were organised, including the 'Workers' Brigade' farms.

Plans soon went awry for various reasons. There were shortages of trained management and technical personnel to run the new state enterprises; many projects were badly thought out and carried out for political rather than commercial reasons. For example, a meat factory was built near Bolgatanga to produce both meat and hides for shoe manufacture even though there was insufficient livestock available in the area for the factory to operate at anywhere near full capacity. Attempts at agricultural collectivisation and mechanisation turned out to be huge economic failures. Management was poor, and although large amounts of capital were spent on this sector, productivity at the collective farms was pitifully low compared to small-scale enterprises. Meanwhile, family farmers and small-scale industries were virtually ignored.

Other developments were more promising, however. The CPP administration invested in health and education expansion, roads, and in the Akosombo dam, a hydro-electric power generation project. Some attempts were made to address the disparities in levels of development between the north and south.

When national savings ran out, the CPP paid for essential imports through domestic and overseas borrowing. Mismanagement and corruption in state-owned enterprises and at collective farms became endemic; by the mid-1960s, debt and inflation were the order of the day,

He who fashions a footpath does not know that behind him it is crooked.

Akan proverb

and an overvalued currency discouraged other countries from buying Ghanaian goods. Earnings from cocoa declined, as foreign competition emerged and world prices fell. Local production fell as a result of the Ghanaian Marketing Board's bureaucratic incompetence and the low prices it paid to farmers. Economic decline had set in.

Meanwhile, Ghana was moving from a newly independent democratic nation to an authoritarian one-party state. Nkrumah had begun to clamp down on political opposition. He pushed through constitutional change which enabled him to be declared President for Life in 1960 and allowed him to appoint his supporters to positions of leadership in the administration, compromising the independent and meritocratic nature of the civil service. In 1964, all parties apart from the CPP were banned.

In 1966, Nkrumah's regime was brought to an abrupt halt. Officers who had felt increasingly dissatisfied with the economic and political situation, staged a coup, encouraged by successful military take overs in various African nations during the 1960s. Nkrumah was out of the country at the time; he never returned to Ghana, living in exile in Guinea. He died in Bucharest, Romania, in 1972.

Nkrumah and Pan-Africanism

Nkrumah's vision extended wider than the achievement of independence for Ghana. During his stay in London, he had played an important part in the Pan-Africanist and anti-colonial movement and met the activists W.E.B. DuBois from the USA and George Padmore from the West Indies. Nkrumah dreamt of a federation of African States (in this context, he saw his own marriage to an Egyptian as a political act). This vision continues to resonate today, in Africa and throughout the diaspora.

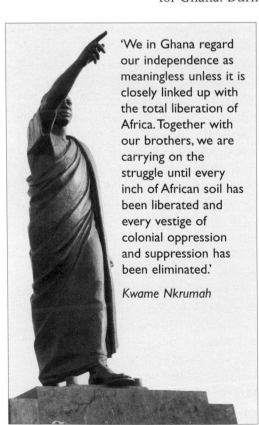

'We in Ghana regard our independence as meaningless unless it is closely linked up with the total liberation of Africa. Together with our brothers, we are carrying on the struggle until every inch of African soil has been liberated and every vestige of colonial oppression and suppression has been eliminated.'

Kwame Nkrumah

Seeing Ghana as the 'Black Star' of Africa, which could spearhead the campaign for independence for all African states, Nkrumah committed national resources to this effort, another factor in causing Ghana's economic misfortunes.

Nkrumah also helped found the Non-Aligned Movement, a grouping of states that tried to pursue political directions independent of the cold-war division between East and West.

Changes of government and economic decline

The military take over which toppled Nkrumah's regime led to three years of government by the National Liberation Council (NLC). The NLC included military personnel and civilians, whose policies were not substan-tially different to those pursued by the CPP.

▲ *Dependence on oil imports worsened the state of Ghana's economy in the 1970s.*

From the start, the NLC planned for a return to civilian rule. In 1968 the ban on political parties was lifted, and democratic elections were held in 1969. The Progress Party headed by Kofi Busia, a brilliant academic whose party had opposed Nkrumah in parliament, won and formed a new civilian administration.

Busia's government inherited a dismal economic situation: large foreign debts; even larger domestic debts which fuelled inflation; falling cocoa revenue. Busia drew up well thought-out austerity measures, including cuts in defence spending, but these were widely unpopular, especially within the armed forces. After two years in government, continued economic problems led to a second coup in 1972, staged under the leadership of Lieutenant Colonel Acheampong.

Acheampong's new National Redemption Council was a wholly military government, reorganised as the Supreme Military Council (SMC) in 1975. They saw an imposition of military organisation on every aspect of life as the solution to Ghana's problems. All ministries and state-owned enterprises were put under the direction of military officers, and no timetable for a return to civilian rule was put forward until 1977.

The SMC regime earned popularity initially because Busia's austerity measures were revoked. When Operation Feed Yourself, a programme to stimulate national self-sufficiency in food, was launched, even students appeared in large numbers to assist at harvest time. But the reversal of economic restraint compounded economic woes: the trend towards decline continued, partly due to external factors. Steep hikes in world oil prices during and after 1974 meant that Ghana was left without fuel, because the country lacked foreign exchange and credit. Food production declined while the population grew. Although world cocoa prices rose later in the 1970s, many cocoa farmers had stopped investing in their farms and could not respond by increasing productivity. Patterns of smuggling across borders, which developed because of low prices paid to farmers in Ghana, also diminished government revenues from cocoa.

Accusations of government corruption began to fly, and the SMC initiated a crackdown on criticism. Independent newspapers were closed down, and journalists detained. The universities, which had become centres of opposition to the regime, were repeatedly closed; student protests were broken up by armed soldiers. There were calls for the restoration of civilian rule, although other shades of opinion were in favour of 'union' government, a mix of military and elected civilian leaders. In a referendum in 1978, the people voted narrowly in favour of union government. But later in the year, the SMC forced Acheampong to resign and placed Lieutenant General Frederick Akuffo in power.

This change of government was prompted by the economic crisis into which Ghana was entering. Basic commodities were in short supply, inflation was estimated at 300 per cent, and cocoa production had dropped to half of the 1964 output. Calls for political freedom continued, as did strikes protesting against the economic and political situation. The government responded by planning for a return to civilian rule, and the ban on political parties was lifted in 1979.

Barely a month before the planned general elections, the first violent coup in Ghana took place: spearheaded by a young Flight Lieutenant, J.J. Rawlings, the Armed Forces Revolutionary Council (AFRC) took power in the name of purging corruption. Heads and close associates of former military governments were executed, but the elections were held at the appointed time, and the AFRC sat back to monitor Dr Hilla Limann's new civilian regime.

Despite improved economic plans, Limann's attempts to turn the crisis around were ineffectual, and corruption continued unabated. Trade Unions began to protest that wages no longer covered even basic food needs. The stage was set for yet another coup.

The revolution and economic crisis

J. J. Rawlings staged his 'Second Coming' on 31 December 1981. This coup was declared a 'revolution' after a radio broadcast in which Rawlings stated that he 'wanted a chance for the people, farmers, workers, soldiers, the rich and the poor, to be part of the decision-making process'. He immediately formed a government known as the Provisional National Defence Council (PNDC), whose cabinet members were mostly civilian, and whose aim was the transformation of Ghanaian society. It was the eighth government since the fall of Nkrumah 15 years earlier.

The new regime pursued a new set of policies, self-styled as 'socialism', which included the formation of revolutionary defence and development committees at village and workplace level, the enforcement of price controls which led to violence against market traders, and the confiscation of money from the bank accounts of the better-off. Partly out of fear of a counter-coup, the PNDC dealt ruthlessly with people it regarded as opposition. Political murders included the famous killing of four high court judges; a committee was later set up to investigate the executions, but its findings did not come to light. This was a time of fear, when people 'disappeared' and no one dared speak out.

Meanwhile the precipitous decline in all sectors of the economy continued, and hardship increased. Basic necessities, agricultural inputs, and spare parts for industry and transport were scarce, because the lack of

▲ *Explaining his policies: Rawlings addressing the crowds in 1983.*

foreign exchange curtailed imports. Workers could not make ends meet because inflation drove up prices faster than wages could keep up with. Thousands of professionals left Ghana for greener pastures. Productivity in all sectors dropped, and social services ground to a halt. In 1961–66, Ghana had been 83 per cent self-sufficient in food, but by 1982 this had declined to 23 per cent. By 1983, the country was in economic crisis. A drought year, there were severe food shortages, and the dry conditions contributed to serious bush fires which decimated trees used in industry. This was also the year in which Nigeria chose to expel foreign workers: one million Ghanaians, extra mouths to feed, arrived home. The protruding collar bones characteristic of the era came to be christened 'Rawlings' chains'.

During the first few years of Rawlings' regime, Ghana's foreign policy sought close relations with Colonel Gadafi in Libya and Thomas Sankara, the populist leader of Burkina Faso. As economic crisis continued, the government sought and failed to obtain help from the socialist bloc. In desperation, it was forced to U-turn and in 1983 began negotiations with the IMF and the World Bank. Subsequently, official foreign policy sought to distance Ghana from socialist or populist regimes.

Structural adjustment

Government discussions with the IMF and the World Bank over Ghana's economic crisis led to a new lending agreement conditional upon Ghana following a structural adjustment programme. This Economic Recovery Programme (ERP) was implemented in two stages. The aim of the first phase was to stabilise the economy through various austerity measures. User charges were introduced into social sectors such as education and health, restrictions were imposed on public spending, and subsidies on items such as agricultural inputs were removed. The results have been long-lasting: mothers, many already extremely impoverished by economic decline, now have to pay for the health-care of their children. Students struggle to pay education fees. Fishermen have to cope with prohibitively high fuel costs, and farmers have to stump up steeply increased fertiliser costs, or do without. Banks saw restrictions imposed on lending, and inflation was tackled by devaluing the cedi, which made imported goods more expensive. There were gains for some ordinary people under this phase of adjustment, although they do not outweigh the losses. For example, prices paid to farmers for certain cash crops were increased in an attempt to stimulate exports.

▼ *Most primary schools in Ghana have no desks and chairs. The costs of school fees, uniforms, and books place education out of reach for many children.*

The second phase of the ERP concerned economic restructuring, involving changes in the state's institutions and practices, in order to slim down the scale of state activities while increasing their efficiency. Public ownership was reduced through privatisation. Many sectors in which the state had held a monopoly were opened up to private competition, and public-sector employment was slashed through mass redundancies. A programme to decentralise the organisation of government services was planned, and services began to be restructured. The financial sector was also opened up in an attempt to stimulate investment and the manufacturing sector, and foreign exchange markets were liberalised.

During the first phase of the ERP, official overseas assistance averaged US$ 430 million annually, more than double that of previous years. In practice, the Ghanaian government was able to compromise on some of the original

STOCKS AND SHARES: FATI'S STORY

Fati Yakubu is a stockbroker with Sterling Securities at the Ghana Stock Exchange. Brought up in a village in the far north of the country where girls' education tends to be a low priority for the community, Fati is certainly unusual. Supported by parents who encouraged their sons *and* daughters to pursue an education, Fati was able to attend secondary school in the north and then read for her BA and MBA degrees at the University of Ghana.

Fati says, 'I was the first local stockbroker with Gold Coast Securities, one of the four licensed brokers in existence, when I started the job in 1994. Now almost all floor traders are Ghanaians.'

Fati contrasts the world of the stock exchange with that of her experience of village life. 'Women dominate floor-trading in Ghana, and no man has ever made me feel inferior at work. It is only a matter of time before women get onto the Boards of Directors. When I visit the village, it is a different ball game: women and men lead different lives there. When you are educated, you take one step outside the women's world but you do not join the men. You can sit with the men, but they will change their conversation. They will not discuss things with you, like local politics, which they feel women should not know about.'

dictates of the structural adjustment plans and go its own way in implementing them. For example, state-owned industries and marketing boards have not been sold off in nearly the numbers or at the rate as envisaged in the IMF's and World Bank's plans. But there was general satisfaction with the progress of the ERP, and in return, US$ 575 million dollars were pledged for the next stage of the programme by international agencies and donors.

The consequences of adjustment

Ghana has been lauded internationally by the IMF and the World Bank as a 'flagship' of success for structural adjustment. Economic indicators have been encouraging since adjustment was introduced: between 1983 and 1987 the economy grew by 6 per cent annually, and inflation fell to 20 per cent. Ghana was even able to pay off more than US$500 million in loan arrears dating back over 20 years. Part of the financial liberalisation were plans for a stock exchange which opened in 1990, creating new investment and fund-raising opportunities.

However, there have been worrying signs on the wider economic front since the mid-1990s. Economic growth has slowed; inflation has increased, peaking at 74 per cent in 1995; the devaluation of the cedi continues. The limited successes have been achieved at the expense of taking on a huge debt burden, storing up problems for the future. While Ghana's debt was a relatively small US$ 1.4 billion in 1980, it had risen to US$ 6.2 billion in 1996, almost as large as the nation's gross national product.

Structural adjustment is largely export-oriented, and it has been successful in boosting gold, cocoa, and timber exports. But this is basically

► Joe Manyanu, eight years old, works on Saturdays weaving kente cloth in order to afford school fees, his uniform, and some books. After work, he likes to play football with his friends.

a reversion to the pre-independence economy, with little concern for investing in high-return industries which add value to raw materials. The government had hoped to stimulate the manufacturing sector, but it has met with little success – rather, opening up businesses to foreign competition has resulted in many local firms closing down. But the government continues to support industry over agriculture, despite the importance and relative success of the latter.

Despite structural adjustment, the economy has not recovered to 1965 levels. The gross national product per head was US$558 in 1965 and only US$370 in 1997. At independence, income per head in Ghana was three times that in Tanzania and double that in Zambia; both countries now outpace Ghana.

At the human level, some things – including food availability – have certainly improved since 1983. As *South* magazine put it in 1997: 'Protruding collar bones, known as Rawlings' chains, have been replaced by protruding stomachs, now known as Rawlings' coats'. It is debatable how far these changes are due to adjustment. In agriculture, for example, farmers have certainly responded to higher prices paid for their export products by increasing output. But the change in weather patterns from the drought year of 1983 to relatively good successive years is also behind improvements in yields, and this increased production has been achieved *despite* new constraints associated with adjustment, which include inflated input prices resulting from subsidy withdrawal and higher prices of imported goods. Constraints also include reduced public spending on agriculture: from 1982 to 1988, spending declined by 4.7 per cent each year.

Most ordinary Ghanaians are yet to see benefits of adjustment in their daily lives, and for many, the economic recovery programme has added to their problems. User charges in the social sectors, such as health-care and school fees, have increased the burden of the poor and reduced service usage. Redundancies, or 'redeployment', in the public and private sectors have led to great hardship amongst the unemployed. It is true that the export sectors that have been stimulated – gold, cocoa, and timber – have expanded and taken on new employees; but the benefits of this opportunity fall mostly to men because few women are employed in these areas. Due to devaluation, costs for vital imported products such as medicine have risen to unaffordable levels, causing serious hardship.

The recent resurgence of inflation has caused suffering especially among wage workers. The value of salaries has been eroded. Because bank interest rates are far below the rate of inflation, savings in cedis are rendered worthless.

▼ *Two observations on the government's attitude to poverty: in 1987, the PNDC introduced a programme to help those in poverty; seven years later, popular cartoonist Ike Essel comments on the 1994 story that state funds were used to pay for a Jacuzzi for Ghana's First Lady – for health reasons.*

'... it is the intention of the Government not to allow perpetual pain bearing to be the core characteristic of the process of adjustment especially as it recognises the considerable length of time over which people have been called upon to endure hardship [...] We believe that adjustment is for the people and not the people for adjustment.'

P.V. Obeng, PNDC member and Chairman of the Structural Adjustment Team, writing in the PAMSCAD policy document, 1987.

Opposition

The early years of the Rawlings' regime bred what became known as a 'culture of silence': little opposition was voiced. Political parties had been banned when the PNDC took power, newspapers were strictly controlled, and the media was state-run and always followed the government line. The government also attempted to curb union and student activity and was accused of political intimidation and human rights abuses. An attempted coup, discovered in June 1982, led to the execution of those implicated.

Opposition to the adjustment programme was initially strongest among unions, lawyers, and students. In 1987, the government planned the Programme of Actions to Mitigate the Social Costs of Adjustment (PAMSCAD), which was designed as a short-term programme and included community, employment creation, basic needs, and education projects. Although PAMSCAD was supposed to tackle the problems of the nation's poorest, who are concentrated in rural northern Ghana, the southern urban areas received the largest share of the funding in order to appease the highly vocal opposition. Rural farmers, especially in the north, find it difficult to organise because of their ethnic and linguistic diversity, lack of unity, dispersed locations, and poor communications.

In the early 1990s, more Ghanaians started to demand a voice. Independent newspapers sprang up and have remained in print more or less ever since, although the government has always prosecuted if it considered a publication libellous. 'Radio Eye', a focus of opposition to government media policy, began broadcasting without a licence. It was immediately shut down. Union membership has been decimated by the level of redundancies. Students continue to protest against government policies, holding major anti-government demonstrations in 1990 and 1993. The universities were closed for a year in 1995, because of a lecturers' dispute over pay.

A particularly contentious adjustment measure was the attempt to increase government tax revenue by introducing value-added tax (VAT). First implemented in 1995, this measure increased prices of basic commodities by 17.5 per cent and sparked off huge inflation. This galvanised opposition in the cities, culminating in massive protests. Two demonstrations in Accra were the largest since Rawlings took power: the first was called Kume Preko, which means 'kill me now', referring to the high level of deprivation. At Kume Preko, security forces shot into the crowd, killing a boy. The second demonstration was then called 'if you've killed me, bury me'. Marchers included teachers and civil servants who felt that the new tax was more than they could bear. There were open calls for Rawlings to step down, which turned the peaceful protest into a battleground between pro and anti-government supporters. Nine people were shot dead and 27 injured. The government withdrew the new tax, but it was reimposed at a rate of 10 per cent at the end of 1988, accompanied by an information campaign explaining the need to raise more taxes. This time, the government exempted certain items including foodstuffs and medicines. These measures made the tax more palatable, and although there have been calls to lower the rate to 5 per cent, VAT has been largely accepted.

Protests against taxes perceived as unjust are nothing new: in the nineteenth century, Ghanaians took to the streets to protest against a poll tax introduced by the British colonial government.

▼ *Three years after the big demonstrations, the government is promoting VAT to its voters via vast billboards.*

Democracy, decentralisation, and development

The PNDC regime developed a remarkable reputation for honesty in its early years. Rawlings waged what he called a 'holy war' on corruption and smuggling, an action which earned him a high degree of popularity. At the same time, he tried to encourage broad-based support: in villages and workplaces, the government fostered the formation of grassroots committees which became known as the Committees for the Defence of the Revolution (CDRs). These were involved in community development projects, anti-corruption surveillance, and in political work in support of the ruling party. Militia wings were also formed, and the government set up public tribunals, outside the ordinary legal system, in order to try those accused of anti-government acts. The transparency and accountability of these tribunals have often been questioned.

At first, Rawlings received much popular support because of his anti-corruption and pro-poor stance. He was thought of as a man of the people, and the media captured this in showing him helping ordinary people to clean drains and to farm. Through the CDRs and their forerunners, he gradually built up a power base at grassroots level.

At the same time, Rawlings developed a group of trusted people who worked in the PNDC administration. Many of these people remain as advisers to the president: they are given official recognition as presidential advisers as members of the Council of State. Set up under the Ghanaian Constitution, appointments to this Council are controlled by the President, and none of the current members are opposition supporters. As public figures associated with the President and the ruling party, members of the Council of State have considerable influence over events in Ghana. Members include Alhaji Mahama Iddrisu, until recently Rawlings' Minister of Defence, and the Chairman Alhaji Mumuni Bawumia.

As opposition grew to the human suffering which accompanied economic adjustment, criticism became more focused on the legitimacy of the military regime itself. During the revolution, Rawlings claimed that his aim was to stamp out corruption, raise the living standard of the poor, and prepare Ghana for democracy. As Ghanaians started to indicate their readiness to participate in politics, the PNDC government saw that transition to democracy was the only long-term option.

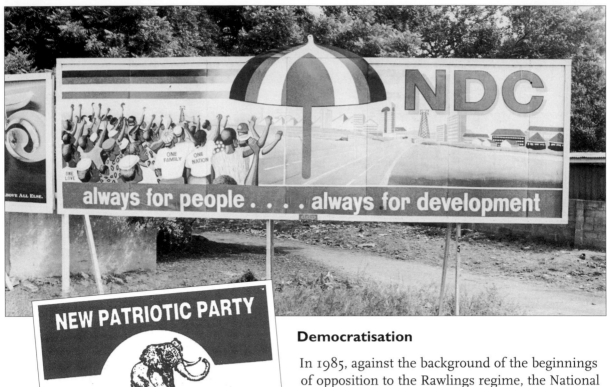

Party slogans and vivid representations of development will return in the 2000 election campaign.

Democratisation

In 1985, against the background of the beginnings of opposition to the Rawlings regime, the National Commission for Democracy was reconstituted to discuss ways of introducing democracy to Ghana. The first stage of democratisation was implemented at the local level: the number of districts was increased to 110, and non-party elections were held in 1988/9 for one-third of the membership of the new District Assemblies. Traditional authorities or their representatives constitute another third, and the final third is made up of political appointees. The political head of the district, the District Chief Executive, is appointed by central government. Because Chief Executives have the final say and former CDR members, committed government supporters, are selected to be prominent in Assemblies, the government can in practice push policy through the Assemblies. The concentration of power in the hands of Chief Executives also permits a lack of democratic accountability.

Meanwhile, as the articulation of political opposition to the government increased, a new national constitution was being drafted. National parliamentary and presidential elections were planned for 1992. Six months before they were held, the ban on party politics was lifted, giving the opposition little time to organise. The opposition parties contesting the elections were basically a continuation of those formed before independence, broadly split along regional and ethnic lines.

The elections were declared free and fair by international observers. Rawlings was elected President, completing the remarkable transition

▲ The former Flight Lieutenant in front of the Ghanaian flag, wearing a kente pattern that denotes unity and democracy, as well as a pilot's watch.

'...for us, democracy cannot simply mean holding ... elections periodically whilst we continue to endure poverty, misery, illiteracy, hunger and poor health facilities and whilst many of our able-bodied citizens are unable to find employment.'

J. J. Rawlings, address to the opening seminar of the National Commission for Democracy, Sunyani, July 1990.

from upstart junior officer to democratically chosen head of state. Allegations of irregularities in voter registration led the opposition to boycott the parliamentary election; as a result, Rawlings' newly renamed party, the National Democratic Congress (NDC), secured almost all the seats. The opposition New Patriotic Party (NPP) branded the result the 'stolen verdict'. Only a minority of independent MPs dared to voice strong criticism of government policy, so this parliament became known as the 'rubber stamp'. A one-party state with Rawlings firmly at the helm remained in place.

The NPP is the largest opposition party and is led by J.A. Kuffour. The NPP opposes the political style of the NDC, regarding the NDC as anti-democratic in the way that opposition marches have been suppressed. Although it agrees that economic adjustment and reform are necessary, the NPP also criticises the NDC's management of structural adjustment, education reform, and the size of the debt burden which is being created.

The general elections in 1996 were less controversial and contested by all parties. Rawlings retained the presidency, and the NDC won a majority in parliament. However, the presence of opposition parties helped foster democratic debate. In a country with widespread illiteracy, using suggestive symbols as markers in advertising and on ballot papers is particularly important. The NDC's symbol is the umbrella which denotes chieftaincy in Ghana, conveying the idea of authority. The symbol of the NPP is an elephant, chosen for its connotations of power and authority (the elephant is seen as chief of jungle animals).

The elections in 2000 will be both presidential and parliamentary: Rawlings is due to stand down at these elections, since under the Constitution an elected President may only serve for two terms. His deputy, Ata Mills, is due to contest as the NDC presidential candidate.

Ethnicity and regional allegiance in Ghanaian politics

There is an ethnic factor in Ghanaian politics in two senses. In terms of voting patterns, the NPP has strong support in the Ashanti and coastal Akan-speaking areas; the NDC has its stronghold in the Volta Region but also attracts wider support. The parties also tend to attract different classes of voter: the NPP is the favoured party of many intellectuals and academics. At the same time, Rawlings is often accused of favouring his mother's ethnic group, the Ewe, in appointments to high office. But many other groups are represented in the cabinet, and the ethnic factor should not be overplayed.

Things are looking good for the future of democracy in Ghana. At the same time, the country's human rights record continues to improve, and the independence of the Ghanaian judiciary has been reasserted.

Decentralisation

The purpose of decentralisation is to replace a centralised system of administration with a form of government that is closer to the people in order to promote their participation in decision-making. It is hoped that this participation will both strengthen democracy and ensure that decisions about development are made in the interests of people at the grassroots. As part of this process, and hand-in-hand with the process of democratisation, government functions are being decentralised. Major decisions on matters such as education are to be made at the district level, rather than by the relevant ministry. Government departments at district level are supposed to co-operate in designing development plans according to local need, in conjunction with District Assemblies and District Chief Executives. In practice, the process of change is slow, since the culture of centralised decision-making is difficult to transform quickly. Moreover, the changes have increased the District Chief Executives' influence on the decentralised departments.

Central government allocates up to 5 per cent of Ghana's total annual income to a District Assemblies' Common Fund, intended to finance development activity. Each Assembly must raise 5 per cent of the funds allocated to it through local market taxes and other revenues, so Assemblies situated in the more prosperous areas of the country are able to raise more development funds and gain greater allocations of central funding. This has resulted in wider development gaps, particularly between the north and the south.

The government has made some notable new departures in infrastructural development in all areas of the country. Most of these are co-financed with donors or are part of donor programmes associated with structural adjustment priorities. They include the National Electrification Scheme, started in 1989, which aimed to take power to the rural areas. By 1998, most district capitals and towns of similar sizes were linked to the national grid. The government has also rebuilt airports and rehabilitated principal trunk roads between major towns, some of which used to become impassable during the rainy season. All these developments have spread the popular appeal of the NDC government. They have also led to narrowing the gap between urban and rural areas and the north and south in terms of infrastructure. But the progress has done little to assist people living in poverty directly – for example, most of the rural poor cannot afford electricity.

▲ The roads might have been improved, but the style of travelling reflects the price of transport to most Ghanaians.

JOSHUA AND THE GHANA SOCIETY OF THE PHYSICALLY HANDICAPPED

Joshua Asiedu, 32, is a tailor and embroiderer. As a disabled person, he faced a lot of discrimination in his early life. 'My parents did not look after me in the same way as they looked after my brothers and sisters. I was able to pass the entrance exam for secondary school but they refused to sponsor me.'

Joshua joined the Ghana Society of the Physically Handicapped, a membership-based NGO, which helped Joshua to train at the Jachie Training Centre for the Handicapped. He is now Head of Tailoring at the Production Centre there.

'The Society was founded by disabled people 18 years ago. It is a national organisation with offices in every region. We don't want handicapped people to have to beg or to be sorrowful so we come together to combat our problems', explains Joshua. The Society also organises sports and other social events, and campaigns for the rights of disabled people. Its members seek to change discriminatory attitudes through educational work: 'Parents disown disabled children in Ghana because they feel the children won't be able to look after them in their old age', comments Joshua. 'It's not true. The Society approaches parents to educate them about this, and attitudes are changing. Disabled people also find it difficult to get accommodation in Ghana because of prejudice. We approach landlords to encourage them to rent rooms to disabled people.'

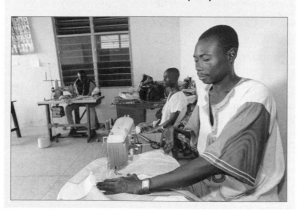

Supplementing the state: non-government organisations (NGOs)

There are many types of non-government organisations working to alleviate poverty and further development in Ghana. Local organisations range from community-based groupings, such as village women's self-help groups which are found all over Ghana, to formally constituted NGOs. These organisations' scope and capacities differ widely: community self-help groups often concentrate on undertaking traditional work tasks and on mobilising savings, but often lack access to credit and skills such as book-keeping and leadership. Local NGOs tend to specialise in particular areas such as health, water, education, disability, or income-generating projects. Some are strong organisations with professional staff; many are affiliated to religious organisations, which informs their approaches to development. This is a very dynamic sector. New organisations appear all the time, and existing agencies change. Grassroots organisations may grow and become formal organisations while others disappear over time.

A number of church-based, Islamic, and secular international NGOs also work in Ghana, operating development projects as well as funding local partner organisations. Again, these are engaged in a variety of areas and have a range of objectives.

Relations with government

NGOs have often operated in isolation in Ghana, but recently, networks of NGOs have begun to appear. The overall umbrella organisation, the Ghana Association of Private and Voluntary Organisations in Development (GAPVOD), keeps a register of NGOs in Ghana and seeks to defend NGOs' interests. Other NGO networks have been created in order to exchange ideas on specific topics and to promote learning. The Northern Ghana Network for Development, for example, works to strengthen the institutional capacity of its member organisations through information-sharing and research. Church-based agricultural projects network to co-ordinate action on a regional basis.

The relationships between these agencies and the state vary: at the local level, where development services are delivered, collaboration between individual agencies and particular government departments is often very good. It is at the national level, in the arena of policy-making, that relations have become strained. In recent years, the government has attempted to introduce a new framework for the registration of NGOs and a new forum for government–NGO dialogue through a new NGO Bill. The government says that this is necessary because of the numbers of 'bogus' NGOs, organisations which operate under the cover of NGO status in order to benefit from tax-free imports and other advantages enjoyed by the charitable sector.

NGOs have resisted these proposals, seeing them as a way in which the government desires to increase its political as well as financial control over the sector. They argue that the Bill proposed changes which conflict with various clauses of the 1992 Constitution, including those which guarantee freedom of association. NGOs claim that the existing registration and regulatory framework would be adequate were it put into practice. GAPVOD does, however, wish to see measures put in place which will improve government–NGO communication, to facilitate NGO activity rather than regulate it.

Although the Bill is no longer officially on the cards, the government continues to put forward the same ideas. At the centre of this debate is the question of the role and identity of NGOs. The government wishes them to fit into its vision of development and complement its own resource-limited development work, while NGOs lobby for alternative development policies. Many NGOs seek to implement donors' visions for development rather than support national policies, and some lack the sensitivity to see that they are encroaching on the domain of an elected government in doing this.

The backdrop to the controversy is the search for funds which inevitably brings NGOs and the government into conflict. NGOs tend to have strong links with international donors and claim that their methods are cheap and effective, so they have often been very successful in contesting for funding. This can cause resentment and grievances in government departments.

Relationships at the national level inevitably vary according to the nature of the NGO. Given the diplomatic and financial backing from some countries to international NGOs operating in Ghana, the government is led to treat these agencies with more respect. There is some positive co-operation. Currently, the World Bank, NGOs, and the government are collaborating on a major review of structural adjustment in Ghana.

It is notably difficult to separate a particular set of local NGOs from the government apparatus itself. The largest of these, the 31st December Women's Movement, formed in the wake of the 1981 revolution, is headed by the First Lady, Mrs Nana Konadu Agyeman Rawlings. The Movement runs many development projects, assisting large numbers of women, and promotes gender equality practically and ideologically. But it is also politically partisan and has helped shore up the political regime through mobilising women's votes.

▲ Languages and cultures cross national boundaries: A hair salon near Kumasi with Akan and French slogans, using the US flag to draw in fashion-conscious ladies.

▼ Adiza Bashiru has come to Ghana from Lagos, Nigeria, to look for work. At a 1999 summit, ECOWAS leaders decided to eliminate obstructions to travel such as border checkpoints between member countries.

Ghana's role in West Africa

Ghana is a founder member of the Economic Community of West African States (ECOWAS) which includes her immediate French-speaking neighbours Togo, Côte d'Ivoire, and Burkina Faso. This is a grouping of 18 countries established in 1975 to promote development through trade, co-operation, and self-reliance. Co-operation achieved in practice does not always live up to the aim, and there is little funding for ECOWAS projects, partly because membership dues are rarely paid. Trade relationships with Western developed countries remain more important to the West African economy than intra-ECOWAS commerce. Ordinary Ghanaians benefit little from ECOWAS, and since Ghana is not part of the francophone West African 'franc' zone, they do not have the advantage of a stable currency either. People find it difficult to save in cash when inflation is high – in Ghana, many people prefer to save in assets from crops to livestock, but these are difficult to convert quickly into cash when needs must be met. In 1999, ECOWAS made a start on the long road to a common currency by announcing the development of a community-wide currency cheque. But although larger traders will be able to take advantage of this, it is having little impact on the majority of Ghanaians who do not have bank accounts.

ECOWAS also sees its peace-keeping role as essential to the development of the region. Ghana has contributed troops to ECOMOG, the

peace-monitoring group which played a significant part in the restoration of peace in war-torn Liberia, and the Ghanaian military had crucial roles in peace-keeping efforts during this eight-year long civil war. As the Chairman of ECOWAS towards the end of the conflict, Rawlings also played a key part in bringing all sides together to negotiate a peace deal. Ghana is currently making a significant contribution to ECOMOG peace-keeping work following bloody civil violence in Sierra Leone.

Oral culture, story-telling, and the media

Greetings

Greetings form an important part of any social encounter in Ghana. They range from a lengthy ritual in a traditional court to a short yet vital 'good morning' in an office environment. Local patterns of greeting vary enormously, depending on the ethnic group, the formality of the occasion, and the relative status of the greeters.

In the Akan tradition, on arriving at a house, people greet all present by handshake in anti-clockwise order, starting with the person on the right. When the new arrivals are seated, the hosts then return this greeting. As with giving, receiving, and signaling, it is considered polite to shake hands with the right hand only. The verbal greeting used, 'akwaaba' or 'welcome', literally means, 'you left and have come back'. In the Dagomba and Mamprusi areas, when greeting a chief, male visitors must squat and clap their hands while female visitors squat and snap their fingers. The chief's official spokesman, the *wudaana*, or 'linguist', often conveys verbal greetings between chief and visitor. The exchange and chewing of kola nuts, a bitter, caffeine-rich nut, are often part of the greeting ritual, although alternative gifts, especially cash, are increasingly offered as 'kola'.

Linguistic display

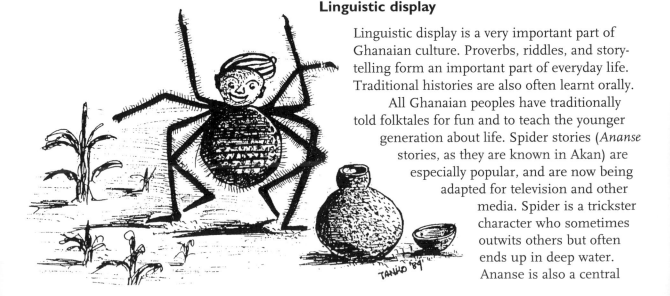

Linguistic display is a very important part of Ghanaian culture. Proverbs, riddles, and story-telling form an important part of everyday life. Traditional histories are also often learnt orally.

All Ghanaian peoples have traditionally told folktales for fun and to teach the younger generation about life. Spider stories (*Ananse* stories, as they are known in Akan) are especially popular, and are now being adapted for television and other media. Spider is a trickster character who sometimes outwits others but often ends up in deep water. Ananse is also a central character in many Caribbean tales, attesting to the cultural linkages between the two regions that exist because of enforced migration through the slave-trade.

In Berekum in the Brong-Ahafo Region, where the Ananse tale related on this page is from, family and friends sit in a circle and take turns to tell stories, from left to right. Everybody gets a chance to entertain and to practise their verbal skills, and the young can learn new stories from the older generation.

In Ghana, people read short stories and satirical pieces in the newspapers with great interest. The greatest exponent of short satire is Kwesi Yankah who writes a column entitled 'Woes of a Kwatriot'. Collections of the pieces are also published in book form, such as *Woes of a Kwatriot: Reflections on the Ghanaian Situation.*

Ghana's most famous novelists include Ayi Kwei Armah, Kojo Laing, and Konadu Asare. Ayi Kwei Armah's celebrated novel *The Beautyful Ones Are Not Yet Born* is set in the last years of Nkrumah's regime. He vividly evokes the disillusion of the time and portrays the central character's struggle with the temptations of corruption. Kojo Laing is a challenging writer who uses prose-poetry to write part-surreal fiction; his novels include *Major Gentl and the Achimota Wars.* Konadu Asare is interested in the inter-woven nature of tradition and modern life in Ghana. Village and town life are brought to life through accessible narrative and intimate characterisation: in *Ordained by the Oracle,* Konadu's main character Boateng has lost his belief in traditions, but after his wife's death he is compelled undergo the Akan 40-day mourning period, during which he recognises the value of traditional customs.

What's in a name?

Naming in Ghana is complex and fascinating. Birth circumstances are an important factor in selecting names: many traditions regard the day of the week on which you are born as significant, and people are known by these birthday names. In northern Ghana, where the days of the week are derived from Hausa (a language related to Arabic), a girl born on Tuesday may be called 'Talata', or 'Lamisi' if she is born on a Thursday. Being a twin is often regarded as spiritually

AN ANANSE STORY

'I have an *Ananse* story to tell you. There lived Kwaku Ananse, his wife, Aso Yaa, and his son NtiKumah. They had a house in a village. One day, Ananse decided, selfishly, that he wanted to be the only wise person in the world. So he took a gourd and went to collect all the wisdom he could find. When he finished putting all the wisdom in the gourd he sealed it up.

Ananse didn't know what to do next, so he decided to hide the gourd on top of a very tall tree, thinking that no one would ever find it there. As he began to climb the tree, NtiKumah stood and watched. Instead of carrying the gourd on his back, Ananse was clutching it to his fat stomach. This made climbing very difficult. NtiKumah suggested, 'Father, wouldn't it be better to carry the gourd on your back to make the climb easier?'

On hearing this, Ananse became annoyed. He thought he had gathered together all the wisdom in the world, so where was this good idea coming from? As his temper got the better of him, he lost concentration, and the gourd fell from his hand. When the gourd hit the ground, it shattered into thousands of pieces and the wisdom it contained scattered all over the world.

And that is how we came to find wisdom everywhere!

I have just ended my Ananse story and whether you like it or not, you should take over.'

In the Mamprusi kingdom, drummers are the custodians of history. Children in drumming families are schooled in the histories by their elders. The histories are sung to the accompaniment of 'talking' drums on formal state occasions. A 'talking' drum allows communication in a drum language. The player squeezes the hour-glass shaped drum under the arm to change the pitch.

Issifu Yacoubu, a farmer and royal drummer at the king's court in Nalerigu, explains: 'The histories tell of creation and of the reigns of previous kings which span more than 500 years. They state the norms and values of society through the use of proverbs and metaphors.' He is teaching his sons Latifu and Harouna to play the drum.

The kings are always praised and their stories are presented in a positive light in the histories, which encourages their descendants to give money to the drummers – the economic side of the occasion!

significant. A twin is called 'Ata' in Ashanti (so the famous Ghanaian writer Ama Ata Aidoo was born on a Saturday as one of twins). In some areas, families arrange for a divination ceremony at the birth of a child; this may reveal that an ancestor spirit has become reborn and so the newborn is named after this ancestor. Naming ceremonies range from Christian baptism and Islamic naming ceremonies to traditional 'outdooring' rituals.

As people age and gain status in Ghanaian society, the names used to address them often change. Respect and seniority are given to the elderly who may be addressed by traditional titles they have acquired or as 'chief' or 'auntie', rather than by birth names. People may take on 'praise names' or names associated with office. Because these names are considered 'heavy' or powerful, they are sometimes used only on ritual occasions, rather than in everyday situations. Praise and office names are often proverbial or historic; for instance, one Mamprusi king chose the name Kparakpiim, 'needle', because he wished to sew the kingdom together. Mamprusi people then had to use alternative ways of referring to needles since the everyday use of 'kparakpiim' became forbidden. The new Ashanti king, enstooled in 1999, has chosen the name Otomfuo Osei Tutu II. This name can be used freely but has an important referent: according to legend, Osei Tutu I, who founded the Ashanti kingdom in 1697, united the Ashanti tribes into one nation. His traditional priest, Okomfo Anokye, conjured the golden stool, which embodies the soul of the Ashanti, from the sky.

AKAN NAMES

In Akan, birthday names are 'soul names', *kra din*. There are practical uses for soul names. It is common for church collections in Kumasi to be held according to soul name, neatly dividing up the congregation!

	Monday	Tuesday	Wednesday	Thursday	Friday	Saturday	Sunday
Female	Adwoa	Abenaa	Akua	Yaa	Afua	Ama	Akosua
Male	Kwadwo	Kwabena	Kwaku	Yaw	Kofi	Kwame	Kwasi

Newspapers and magazines

Printed media are mainly distributed and read by Ghana's urban population: circulation is low due to transport problems and illiteracy. But in the cities, titles such as the *Daily Graphic* and the weekly *Public Agenda* compete for readers, offering news, political comment (often in the form of cartoons), and a plethora of moral advice. Even leader columns in the national dailies may give such advice, and most newspapers have a least one page on moral and religious questions. Another interesting facet of Ghanaian newspapers is the space taken up be funeral announcements, thanks to mourners for their 'sympathy' (including monetary contributions) at recent funerals, and announcements of anniversaries of deaths (mostly after a year and ten years). The style of these announcements is fascinating: for a funeral, there is usually a large photograph with the title, name, and sometimes nickname of the deceased. Then the chief mourners are listed, each with their honours, place of work, and place of residence. The children, nephews, and nieces are then detailed with the same information. Funeral announcements read as a who's who in terms of which people the deceased is connected to, rather than what his or her personal achievements are. Their status is reflected in the positions of others within the clan, and the advertisement also reads as a clan roll call in a time when clan members may live in different places around the world.

▼ *Selling newpapers at Kejetia Market, Kumasi.*

Film, theatre, and television

Films made for video in local languages are becoming increasingly popular in Ghana. Their most enduring themes are marriage and the supernatural. Video films are accessible to people even in small towns: there is usually a 'video house' open to the public for low charges, run by an entrepreneur who has invested in a generator, television, and video. Imported Chinese action films and Indian Bollywood movies are also popular.

Plays are performed at the National Theatre in Accra and in the Cultural Centres in Accra, Kumasi, Tamale, and other cities. Comedians also perform at these venues and in smaller towns. The Ghanaian Broadcasting Corporation (GBC) broadcasts plays in English and other languages. *Concert Party*, televised in Akan, attracts the largest audiences. *Concert Party* warms up with a comedian and has a morality play as its centrepiece, often performed by drama groups affiliated to churches. These plays' recurring theme is the negative influence of Western lifestyles on Ghanaian life. Ironically, GBC also broadcasts many cheap and low-quality Western situation comedies which enjoy equal popularity.

▼ *A cameraman is filming a festival in Cape Coast. At the other end of the country, DJ Idi Abdulai is working in the Radio Progress studio, which is soundproofed with egg boxes.*

Radio

Radio is the most accessible medium in Ghana, because sets are relatively affordable and found in the most remote areas. The GBC produces news, entertainment, and educational programmes in English and seven Ghanaian languages. Since private radio stations were first licensed in the early 1990s, local FM stations transmitting in a wider range of languages have sprung up all over Ghana: commercial stations broadcasting news, discussion, and music; development-oriented community stations, such as Radio Progress in Wa, often funded by the voluntary sector; and FM stations set up by the GBC. This diversity in radio broadcasting has brought a new way of knowing about and engaging with the world to people who had little experience of relatively open 'talk radio'.

The basics:
health and water

The economic crisis in Ghana severely weakened the already limited health-care system. Investment ceased, repair and running costs could not be met, and salaries were slashed. Services broke down as equipment failed, the most basic drugs became unobtainable, and staff morale plummeted. Qualified staff voted with their feet: it is estimated that over half of Ghana's doctors had left the country by 1983.

The economic recovery attributed to adjustment has undoubtedly contributed to the system's revival. Government spending on health in real terms fell by 80 per cent between 1975 and 1983, but had risen above 1975 levels by 1990. Yet adjustment also imposed new costs on patients: doctors and clinics started charging 'user fees' for treatment and drugs as a way of raising revenue for health care. Since salaries have not even recovered their 1975 levels, staff suffer low morale and are tempted to impose unofficial 'under-the-counter' charges to make ends meet. As a result, health services have become inaccessible for the poorest in Ghana.

People may use traditional health-care practices (many of which are effective) but if people who are poor need to buy pharmaceuticals, they are forced to rely on untrained drug peddlers who will sell on credit. These peddlers deal in all types of pharmaceuticals, regardless of the prescription rules and recommended dosages; serious health problems are an inevitable result.

▼ *Women and girls usually bear the brunt of cuts in social services, because they are expected to look after the family's wellbeing: if there is no well near the village, women walk long distances to fetch water.*

Decentralisation

Adjustment in the health system has provided a window of opportunity for change. Previously a system where policy was imposed within a strict hierarchy almost regardless of local need, the Ministry of Health has begun to decentralise planning. At an early stage, this provides hope for the future – but decentralisation has not yet

'I BEG TO PAY WHAT I CAN': AKIBISE'S STORY

Akibise Amantira lives with her husband, co-wife, and four of her children in a village in the Upper East Region. When Akibise or her children get sick, she is expected to pay for the costs of health care, although sometimes her husband contributes. Akibise occasionally uses the local Ministry of Health clinic, but in an emergency she cannot go there at short notice, because under the 'cash and carry' drug-supply system, the cost must be paid up front.

'In the case of severe sickness, I usually go to the drug peddler', says Akibise. 'I beg to pay what I can afford at the time and work to fetch firewood from the bush to sell so that I can pay back the rest of the debt. Another reason why I go to the peddler is that he is always there. The clinic nurse is often not around.'

been matched by a redistribution of funding. Ghana inherited a colonial health system which focused on high-quality expensive hospital care. Today, the two teaching hospitals in the south of Ghana continue to receive 20 per cent of all health funding; less than 0.5 per cent of non-wage expenditure reaches the primary health-care centres. Spending is also lower in the north of the country.

Problems, patterns, solutions

Prevalent health problems in Ghana include a high infant mortality rate which can be attributed to a lack of basic hygiene education, poor sanitation, inadequate reproductive health care, low child-vaccination rates, and malnutrition. The most prominent disease in Ghana by far is malaria: in 1995 alone, 1,175,000 cases were reported, but because most people who suffer from malaria resort to self-medication, this is likely to be a gross underestimate. In the absence of a malaria vaccine, environmental improvements are required to check mosquito breeding. In a country where open drains are the norm, even in Accra, there has been little progress in malaria control. As resistance to common anti-malaria drugs increases, the problem worsens. The illness is responsible not only for deaths but also for thousands of work hours lost through its debilitating effects.

Other diseases include tuberculosis (10,449 cases reported in 1996), measles, and periodic epidemics of meningitis; cholera,

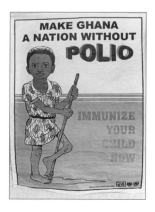

▶ *Health centres use colourful, simple posters to fight disease.*

guinea worm, and river blindness are major waterborne diseases. All these infections are associated with poverty. HIV and AIDS are thought to be growing problems, and it was estimated that 2.38 per cent of adults had the HIV infection in 1997. The government is pursuing a strong public awareness campaign on HIV and AIDS, attempting to change people's behaviour in order to prevent a repetition of the epidemics seen in eastern and southern Africa. It is difficult to assess its success, and Ghana is estimated to have the second highest rate of HIV infection in West Africa.

Sickness can have a terrible immediate impact on a family. While those who work in the public sector get some help with hospital charges, the majority of Ghanaians have no safety net beyond the help they may get from their families. In order to pay for transport to hospital and health fees, a patient's family's savings may be wiped out, so they must borrow money, or sell property. In turn, they will have less money to pay for food, school fees, and to meet other basic needs. If there are delays in raising cash, the patient's treatment is deferred, he or she suffers more pain, and has lower chances of recovery. Choosing between many urgent priorities, families may have to decide not to seek treatment at all.

For breadwinners employed outside the formal sector, sickness may lead to an immediate loss of earnings, jeopardising the family's food security. Small-scale farmers' families often experience ill health when food begins to run out after a poor harvest, and poor nutrition increases their susceptibility to disease, yet it is just during this 'hunger time' at the beginning of the agricultural season when most strength is required to clear and plant land. Thus, a single bad harvest can set off a vicious circle of seasonal ill health and malnutrition. Ill health and poor nutrition affects not only work but also all other areas of life: for children, school attendance and performance are a major casualty.

▼ *Health workers Mariama Sumani and Rebecca Challey are talking about a woman's project to Zachariah Sandow, regent chief of Kukwa village, and Martha Issah, a nurse. The chief says, 'we are all sharing the task of survival, we each contribute what we can, and then all benefit from the results.'*

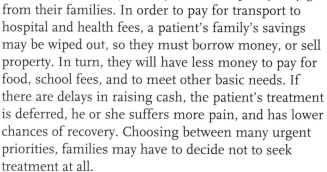

CLEAN WATER

Mariama Sandow and her family are one group of people who have experienced the benefits of safe water, not just in terms of improved health. Mariama lives in Kukwa, a small village that is cut off from the rest of Ghana by flooding during the rainy season. Mariama farms and parboils rice for a living. In Kukwa, it is the job of women to fetch water for daily needs. Until recently, the water supply for Kukwa was a river. Mariama describes how a new well has changed things: 'We used to walk 2km to fetch dirty water from a river which contains guinea worm. Because of the new well we now have clean water, and because it is nearer, we now have more time for our other work.'

The Ghanaian government has won some victories in the fight against local health problems: village traditional birth attendants have received additional training in 'modern' midwifery methods under a Ministry of Health scheme, which has alleviated some reproductive health problems. Popular posters distributed all over Ghana educate villagers on all kinds of health-care subjects. A campaign against debilitating guinea worm, passed on through contact with contaminated water, has drastically reduced infection rates. Health workers have visited villages advising people not to enter water supplies, such as streams, when infected, and to use filtered water, with filters provided as part of the campaign.

Onchocerciasis (river blindness), another serious condition spread via water, has also been tackled in recent years, and its incidence has been dramatically reduced. However, this was done through aerial spraying of water sources; a stop to spraying is likely to lead to a resurgence of the disease because village-level control measures have not been put in place.

The government and charity sectors are also addressing water-related health problems by constructing safe water sources such as covered wells and boreholes. There is a long way to go, but the proportion of the population with access to safe water has improved considerably, from 35 per cent in 1975 to 56 per cent in 1995.

Education for all

Under the government's 'Vision 2020' development plans, the educational target is 'free compulsory and universal basic education for children of school-going age by the year 2020', but there is a long way to go before it can meet this goal. Under adjustment, the government introduced school fees, which – coupled with the costs of school books and uniforms – have prevented many families from sending children to school. The school enrolment rate of 44 per cent has actually fallen below the 1970 level of 52 per cent.

Cultural reasons also prevent balanced school enrolment and attainment. While 49 per cent of boys attend school, the rate is only 38 per cent of girls, a huge disparity. Adult literacy rates stand at 64 per cent for men and 42 per cent for women, and there are extreme regional differentials: in northern Ghana, women's literacy is estimated at less than 5 per cent.

Nevertheless, Ghanaians do place great value on education and are willing to make great sacrifices to ensure that they and their children benefit from the schooling available. Students and university teachers also

▼ *Joshua Abagna runs the government-sponsored adult literacy and numeracy classes in Zuo village. Since 1997, there have been classes specifically for women.*

WORKING TO PAY FOR SCHOOL: FADILA'S STORY

Fadila al Hassan, aged 15, is a junior secondary pupil in Tamale. Fadila's father is able to pay her school fees, the equivalent of US$3.20 a term (the average minimum wage in Ghana is less than US$32 a month). But school uniforms and books are expensive, so Fadila hawks 'ice water' at the bus station and on the main road. Fadila buys the plastic bags of iced water from a wholesaler and can make about 80 cents if she works for a whole day. She works every day after school, all weekend, and during the school holidays.

play an important role in national political life, voicing opposition to the government when others have not dared to speak out.

The years of economic decline took their toll on the education system; shortages of books, equipment, and teachers remain endemic. School buildings are in disrepair and often lack even basic furniture, and teacher salaries are low: pupil-teachers, the backbone of the primary system, earn the equivalent of US$44 a month. Teachers therefore not only suffer low morale but must inevitably find other ways of earning an income, which reduce the time they can spend teaching and preparing lessons. Where parents can afford it, sending their children to one of the many private preparatory schools has become a priority. But the majority of children study in overcrowded and poorly equipped state schools.

Restructuring: a curriculum for development?

After being affected by economic adjustment, the next change to hit the education system was sweeping school reform. The old 17-year system of education, which emphasised the attainment of a narrow range of passes in academic subjects at O- and A-levels, was replaced with a 12-year system based on the US model. The new system emphasised a more wide-ranging education and included vocational studies at the junior secondary level. This shift in emphasis provoked a huge debate in Ghana about appropriate schooling: supporters of the changes said that the old system was outmoded and not suited to the country's real needs. It bred a small elite and a large number of drop-outs with no suitable training for any kind of work, whereas what Ghana needed was vocational training for economic development. Opponents said that the new system would breed a nation of artisans and that Ghana should not settle for that – what Ghana really needed was an expanded academic system.

Ghana has ended up with a combination of both approaches, but suffers from underfunding in all sectors. The creation of new junior and senior secondary schools outpaces the resources available for buildings, equipment, teachers, and books, and yet, the provision is still insufficient for Ghana's rapidly expanding young population. At the tertiary level, a new university was created in the north, and enrolment was expanded at the other four. Degree courses have also been extended to four years to maintain standards, but extreme overcrowding and strong pressure on university resources have been the result. As an adjustment measure, tuition and boarding fees have been introduced. For many students, paying the newly imposed university fees was already a struggle, and poor school-leavers were particularly discouraged from applying.

But in 1998, the government proposed a sharp increase. The national student's union protested against this idea, and in 1999, there were protests on campuses around the country. The largest protest took place in Accra and ended in violent clashes between students and police. The government then held talks with student leaders and parents and suggested the creation of a C3 billion fund for needy students as a way out of the impasse. Student leaders argued that this sum was inadequate but the government maintained that most university students come from relatively well-off families. However, the students also warned that, in practice, the special assistance would not be distributed according to need. Some students have started paying the new fees, and three universities continue as normal. This has given the government room for manoeuvre,

BOWKU, A RURAL PRIMARY SCHOOL

Bowku is a typical village in northern Ghana. It has a six-classroom primary school built by the community. Three of the rooms are thatched. The other three are covered with zinc roofing sheets provided by the government. There are few chairs or other equipment; the blackboard is made from torch battery fluid spread on the wall. Some children take their own stools to school.

Bowku school has two teachers, educated to middle school level, who teach the six classes in the school. The teachers estimate the enrolment rate to be less than 40 per cent. Both teachers live in the village and are able to assist the younger pupils in their own language. Since wages are low, both the teachers supplement their income with farming.

FATAIYA'S PLANS FOR THE FUTURE

Fataiya Issifu is 15 and has been profoundly deaf since the age of 8 following a fever. There was no provision for her special educational needs in her home area. Six years ago, her mother heard about Savelugu School for the Deaf which provides education from nursery to junior secondary levels. The school is open to all, and tuition and lodging are paid for by the government. Since joining the school, Fataiya has learned to sign as well as to read and write. She studies the full range of junior school subjects and hopes to gain admission to one of the two secondary schools for the deaf in Ghana to learn tailoring.

Fataiya signs, 'I am very happy here and the school has benefited me a lot. I will try for a place at secondary school next. With training from there I will be able to get a good husband to marry!'

but the University of Ghana campus at Legon remains closed due to the student unrest.

The ongoing dispute is a dilemma for Ghana. Poorer students will inevitably be excluded from degree-level study as fees increase. Fati Yakubu, the stockbroker who tells her story on p25, would not have got to where she is without free education. At the same time, because of constraints imposed by structural adjustment, there is simply not enough money available to educate Ghanaians to a good standard. Ghana's decision-makers must make difficult choices about the distribution of funding between the primary, secondary, and tertiary sectors. Some argue that since higher education accounts for about a third of the total education budget but is only enjoyed by a few thousand students a year, subsidy cuts are most equitably made there. But this focus on benefits to individuals forgets the important role that these few, well educated Ghanaians can play in the country's future development. Indeed, anything but an increase in the quality and quantity of education at all levels in Ghana is to mortgage the future of the next generation.

Education for all?

Despite the lack of resources, there is some provision for adult and special-needs education in Ghana.

The Non-Formal Education Division of the Ghana Education Service runs innovative programmes to encourage adult literacy in local languages, in conjunction with radio and television support. The new Radio Savannah FM station in the north, for example, receives 50 per cent of its funding from this Division. Its broadcasts try to encourage literacy while educating learners on development issues from health and water to civil rights. This programme aims to fulfil another ambitious aspect of Vision 2020: to eradicate adult illiteracy in Ghana.

Living off the land

Agriculture is the most important economic sector in Ghana. Over half the population are employed in farming, and agricultural products make up 45 per cent of national income (GDP).

Systems of land tenure and access

Many agricultural problems are tied up with systems of tenure and access. Land-related law and actual practice diverge, often to the disadvantage of people who live in poverty. The state owns some land, notably vast forest and nature reserves, but most land in Ghana is vested in clans, and traditional authorities have a strong influence over land matters. In accordance with tradition, a person's access to land is largely determined by patterns of inheritance. Some people may buy and sell land according to government land law, but this mostly applies to urban land for building and agricultural land for cash-cropping.

In the rural areas of northern Ghana, land is seldom bought and sold. Those who do not control farming land must 'beg' for it. Land-holders are unlikely to permit long-term access to a particular plot, discouraging land improvements and tree-planting. Women, who do not inherit land, are placed at a particular disadvantage. It also affects young male farmers and immigrants, but while local young men will eventually get permanent access through division of lineage land to which they are entitled, immigrants find it hard to get land of their own.

In the south, there is a greater market in land. But here, some clan heads have used their positions to sell land for their own gain, and disputes over titles to land are endemic. It is easier for people to get ownership rights to land through purchase, but this is beyond the reach of the poor. Immigrant farmers often enter a sharecropping scheme. There are two common forms. Under *abunu*, the landowner and the operator share proceeds of the sale of the crop equally. This system is more often used for annual crops. Under *abusa*, the operator receives a third of the proceeds but as the scheme covers tree crops which have a long gestation, the operator takes the entire profits from the first five seasons in order to recoup the start-up costs. Through either scheme, immigrant farmers may eventually save enough money to buy land.

▲ *In this area, if you want to farm, you must apply to the land committee.*

▼ *Ploughing is usually done by men; women must ask for or hire their services.*

In Akan societies, women can inherit land, but the system is predominantly matrilineal: a woman inherits from her maternal uncles. A woman will work on and improve land belonging to her husband's family, but if he dies, the land will be inherited by his sister's children. The new Law of Intestate Succession seeks to address these problems by assuring that where there is no will, wives and children are made the beneficiaries of an estate. However, it is generally only the well-informed and relatively wealthy who know about and can make use of this legislation. For most widows, their future depends on the kind of relationship they have built up with their in-laws over the years. If the woman is regarded as a 'good wife' to her husband's family – implying that she has shared with them and helped them – one of the sisters' sons will offer to marry the widow and care for her children. On the other hand, if the relationship is bad, the widow will be treated badly by her in-laws during *kunadie*, the forty-day mourning period, and after this period she is likely to leave the house or be turned out from it, to return to her parents' home.

The story of rice

The 1970s saw a boom in large-scale rice production. Credit was available as part of a German-Ghanaian development programme, and the wealthy, who were were able to offer collateral for the loans and to exert an influence on loan allocations, saw it as an opportunity to make money. But in order to justify the capital investment in producing rice, growers need the assurance of long-term land tenure. Some farmers persuaded chiefs to give them permanent access in return for a financial reward; others were able to use their knowledge of the state land registration system to register their purchases legally. Rural dwellers, who regarded the land as theirs, felt dispossessed in this process. Rice-burning was one form of protest.

While some entrepreneurs made large profits from rice, other farmers had problems marketing their rice because no new system had been set up to cope with the vast expansion in production. But the loans still had to be repaid, so those who were unable to sell their rice got into severe financial trouble.

Rice cultivation is currently very profitable. Marketing remains in the hands of private entrepreneurs who have developed efficient domestic marketing. The sector is dominated by large-scale growers, but more recently, government agricultural programmes have helped small numbers of peasant farmers to cultivate rice using up-to-date techniques.

Land and environment

Ghana is facing serious environmental problems. Severe deforestation in the tropical rainforest zone as a result of commercial and illegal logging has resulted in the destruction of 97 per cent of these forests. Government control measures are in place, but much of the biodiversity is already destroyed, and the long-term environmental impact can only be guessed at. At the same time, desertification is affecting the northern zone. This problem crosses national borders: one of its causes is the reduction of tree cover in Burkina Faso. But poverty in northern Ghana has also caused people to over-exploit the land and cut down the trees. Rural women often cut firewood or make charcoal to sell in small towns or to buyers from the large cities, just to make ends meet.

Along the coast, sea encroachment has become a major problem as a result of illegal sand winning which destroys the structures of sand dunes, making them vulnerable to erosion. Both fishing villages and roads along the coast are threatened.

In the mining areas, water poisoning is a major problem. At Obuasi, high levels of arsenic associated with the gold industry have been detected in drinking water sources.

Food crops

Food staples grown in Ghana include yam, cassava, plantain, rice, maize, millet, guinea corn, beans, and groundnuts. Common vegetables include tomatoes, onions, okra, pepper, garden eggs, and types of spinach. Some foods are also gathered from the wild including shea nuts, vegetables, and mushrooms. As you move northwards, rainfall is lower and falls in a single rainy season, and soils are less rich. Here, root crops are cultivated but pulses and cereals begin to dominate the cuisine.

The extension services run by the Ministry of Agriculture offer technical advice and access to inputs to farmers who grow food crops, although more support has been given to cocoa farmers because of the crop's export value. Because both extension and credit services have been

> When a woman is hungry she says, 'Roast something for the children that they may eat.'
>
> *Ghanaian proverb*

► *Abaa Ayariga is making shea nut butter. First she cracks the nuts, and, after frying the kernels, grinds them into a thick brown paste. Water is added, and the mixture beaten and formed into balls, which are heated. As the balls cool, the oil separates and rises to the top. It is skimmed off and left in a cool place until it sets into butter. Shea butter is an important commodity in northern Ghana: it is used in cooking, for medicinal purposes, and skin protection.*

biased towards male and larger-scale farmers, women and the poorest farmers have benefited less from technical improvements available.

Most food crops are grown by small-scale farmers as individuals or on household farms. Some crops, such as vegetables and pulses, are particularly associated with women's production, whereas cereals and root crops are often grown by men or on household farms. Most food processing is undertaken by women – a huge task involving demanding physical labour, water-fetching, and firewood collection.

▲ *Yams for sale.*

What's in a yam?

The yam is a staple food in much of Ghana. Some varieties are among the few crops grown in Ghana which are indigenous to West Africa. Not only crucial to the diet, the yam is also central to the division of labour and the agricultural and ritual calendars in rural communities.

Yam cultivation is not mechanised: when the early rains begin, men raise mounds with short-handled hoes and plant a segment of yam tuber in each. Yams need to be weeded, and both men and women perform this task during the six to seven-month growing season. In the spaces between the mounds, women grow soup ingredients such as pepper or okra, making good use of the labour that men invested in tilling the soil for the mounds. The soup ingredient plants take nutrition from different depths of the soil, so they do not compete with the yams for nutrients. At the same time, they provide some shade for the sprouting yams.

During the harvest, men lift the tubers, and women headload them to the storage area. Yams are often stored above the ground in purpose-built racks, *aputuo*, made from branches and ropes. *Aputuo* can preserve yams for a season, preventing rotting and unwanted germination.

Although the harvest is underway, no one may eat the new yam until after the yam festival. In Nsonsomea, a Brong village, the trad-itional priest and elders decide when the festival should begin. They are under pressure – it is the 'hunger season', and people are anxious to start eating the new crop! Everyone is relieved when the time of the festivities is announced.

On the eve of the celebrations, the traditional priest dances through-out the night and foretells what is in store for the village during the year, both good and bad. To prevent the bad he tells people to 'sweep' it out of the town. On the first morning of the festival, the Nsonsomea residents make an early start. Women and children clean the village. They say that

▲ *Unusually, this cook is pounding and turning the fufu on his own.*

RECIPE FOR LIGHT SOUP AND FUFU

Boil chopped beef or goat meat in a small amount of water, adding one chopped onion, a clove of garlic, and ginger and salt to taste. After four minutes, add more water, tomato paste, and red pepper to taste. After a further ten minutes add one stock cube. Continue boiling until foaming disappears and the meat is well cooked.

Serve with *fufu* made by pounding cooked plantain and yam or cassava until it is a smooth, starchy paste. Alternatively, *fufu* can be made from *fufu* powder available in specialist supermarkets or from instant potato powder, by adding extra dried starch (farina).

they have 'swept the sickness out of the town' and symbolically block the paths leading to the settlement with branches to prevent its return. Shrines to local deities and ancestors are then brought out and washed. New yams are cooked and mashed with red oil. The traditional priest visits all the shrines, sprinkling the yam on the shrines. Sacrifices are made. At last people can begin to eat the new yam and really enjoy the week-long celebrations.

Yam is versatile. It can be boiled, fried, and roasted, but most often it is made into *fufu*. *Fufu* can be prepared from cassava, cocoyam, or plantain and is often made from a combination of cassava and one of the others. Women are usually responsible for *fufu* preparation for the evening family meal. After lighting a charcoal or wood cooking fire, women first prepare soup. There are various delicious flavours; the most popular are groundnut, palm nut, and light soup. Soups are made with meat or fish when available, but a tasty alternative is giant mushroom soup. Freshwater snail soup is an acquired taste. As the soup boils, a charcoal stove must be constantly fanned to maintain the temperature. The tubers are then peeled, sliced and boiled, and reserved for pounding.

Fufu is pounded with a huge pestle and mortar. It usually takes the energy of two to pound, one standing and powering the pestle downwards in rhythmic thumps with full bodily force, and one sitting at the mortar, turning the *fufu* between strokes of the pestle, and introducing more cooked tuber, expertly avoiding crushed hands. This is the time when young men participate, taking control of the pestle as the woman 'drives' the *fufu* in the mortar.

Fufu is served in earthenware bowls with soup. Eaten with the right hand, the *fufu* is rounded into small balls, dipped in the soup, and swallowed without chewing. Eating is a sociable occasion. Friends and family often share the same bowl of food, and visitors are invited to eat with their hosts. Some food is always reserved in the house in case there are visitors later in the evening.

LUCIA'S STORY:
TAKING CARE OF THE EXTENDED FAMILY

Lucia Pupunaa lives at Sambo and is in her late forties. She has five children and is widowed. As custom demands in the Sambo area, Lucia has married her deceased husband's younger brother. As he is blind and has found it difficult to provide food for her and the children, Lucia must meet most of their needs. In addition, Lucia's sister, also a widow, looks to Lucia for help for herself and her children. Lucia's oldest son has migrated south, and his wife is also dependent on Lucia.

Lucia uses a variety of income-generating strategies to make ends meet and to spread the risks. Together with her sister and the children, she works a rice, millet, and bean farm. Lucia also brews local millet beer for sale with the help of her daughter-in-law, while her sister makes and retails charcoal to contribute. Finally, the family rear animals and the women collect shea nuts for sale.

Lucia belongs to a women's group which is assisted

by a local development charity called SOFIDEP. Through the group, Lucia has been able to obtain loans to build up a rice parboiling business. The small profits have helped her to buy food and to afford school fees for her two youngest children. She is able to get by, but she has not been able to pay school fees for all her children, to afford health-care fees, or other things she regards as 'extras'. Lucia says, 'There is nothing better than to cater for your children.'

Yams may be central to rural social life but yam-dependent diets can lead to malnutrition. Whereas cereals contain essential proteins and other nutrients, yams are a relatively poor food. In Ghana, public health promotions of varied diets have reduced the incidence of malnutrition associated with yam diets.

Food security

Areas of northern Ghana have suffered chronic food insecurity, caused by a combination of environmental and historical factors. The effects of unpredictable rainfall and soil erosion and infertility are exacerbated by unsustainable land-use practices, including deforestation and inorganic farming. Because population density is high, land is scarce, but at the same time there is a shortage of men's and young people's labour due to migration. There are few alternative opportunities to earn an income because of the region's underdevelopment, and poverty prevents both agricultural investment and food purchases when there are shortages.

Small-scale farmers, who make up most of the northern population, experience a 'hunger period' before the new harvest, yet maximum energy is required for farming at this time. Men are responsible for providing cereals for the women of the house to cook for the main meal; women provide the other ingredients and the other meals. When the household cereal runs out, women become the food providers of last resort.

Cash crops for export

Most small-scale farmers also grow crops for sale. Ghana's principal export crops are cocoa, coffee, palm oil, cultivated in the south, and rice, cultivated all over Ghana. New, non-traditional exports include pineapples, cashew, cotton, and shea nuts (shea butter is used in manufacturing cosmetics). The small-scale sector produces the bulk of Ghana's export crops, and employs about 55 per cent of the work force.

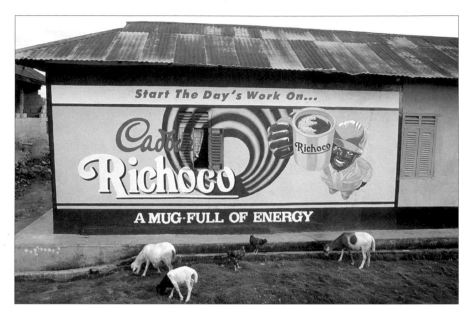

► *A cheerful message; but world prices for cocoa may continue to decline.*

COCOA'S UPS AND DOWNS

Asamoah Serebour has a 6-acre cocoa farm. The drop in cocoa prices and lack of availability of inputs in the early 1980s hit him hard. He welcomes the recent increase in producer prices but finds that prices have not risen as fast as living costs. Asamoah has recently joined a co-operative in his village which is part of Kuapa Kokoo ('best farmer'). Kuapa is one of the new buying companies. Kuapa is able to buy cocoa at higher prices than the state-owned Marketing Board because it exports to 'fair trade' chocolate manufacturers in Europe. Profits are distributed among farmers.

Cocoa, mainstay of the Ghanaian economy

Cocoa has been Ghana's major export for most of this century. Government services and the country's development have largely been paid for through taxes on this sector. In the 1960s, Ghana was the world's largest cocoa producer with an average annual output of 450,000 tonnes, but with a decline in world cocoa prices and the continuing need for the government to tax production, prices paid to farmers fell. As a result of the foreign exchange crisis in the late 1970s, imported inputs such as pesticides became unavailable. Production dropped to a low of 159,000 tonnes in 1983/4, a drought year when forest fires also took their toll on cocoa output. Following an increase in prices paid to farmers under structural adjustment, by 1995 production had recovered to near 1960s levels.

Before adjustment, the state-owned Cocoa Marketing Board controlled all aspects of production, prices, and extension services. Limited liberalisation then allowed private traders to buy cocoa from farmers at competitive prices; the Board itself was 'streamlined', and thousands of its employees were made redundant.

The contribution of cocoa to export earnings has declined from 53 per cent in 1983 to 34 per cent in 1998. But it remains a huge share, and Ghana's dependence on this single crop continues.

Cotton, an up-and-coming cash crop

Cotton production is booming in the north of Ghana. Previously a small sector under the auspices of the national Cotton Development Board, liberalisation has led to the proliferation of private cotton companies. They provide inputs on credit to small-scale growers and buy the crop at the end of the season. One result of this expansion is an increase in women's participation: whereas the former Board biased its extension services towards men, the new cotton companies are commercially oriented and, finding that some of their highest producers are women, they are keen to promote women's production. Traditions have restricted women's access to credit, ploughing, and farm labour, but cotton companies provide assistance with these. Women have also found land access a problem, but because land becomes more fertile after cotton is grown, men are often willing to lend them land for a year's cotton production.

However, cotton expansion also brings environmental problems: in the long term, the crop decreases soil fertility, and fertilisers and pesticides can contaminate water sources.

Most cotton farmers do not get rich but use the proceeds to get by. Some even have to divert some of the inputs such as fertiliser and pesticides to food crops to ensure that enough is produced. Like cocoa, the sector is vulnerable to fluctuations in world prices.

FAMILY AND FARMING: ASIETU'S STORY

Asietu Zibilum lives in northern Ghana and has six children. She works on a farm operated by her husband and his brother. Using grain produced on

their farm, she takes turns with her brother-in-law's wives to cook for the members of the household in the evening. Asietu must provide the 'soup ingredients' for this meal and the food for her children's other meals.

To meet her responsibilities, Asietu cultivates a wide range of crops including okra, leafy vegetables, groundnuts, and black-eyed beans for the family's consumption and for sale to buy essentials. Three years ago, Asietu also began growing cotton. The credit scheme has enabled Asietu to afford inputs which it would have been impossible to purchase up-front. It has also allowed her to get bullock ploughing done on time, even though ploughing for women has a low priority in her village.

Asietu has used profits from cotton to buy food for herself and her children during the 'hunger season', which she thinks has got worse in recent years. Asietu says that women have increasingly had to provide for the family during the hunger season, but sees a glimmer of hope for the future: 'We are suffering these days. But if a man brings food in *and* his wife provides food, together they can solve any problem.'

Minerals, manufacturing, and industry

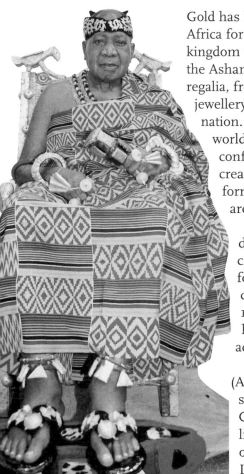

Gold has been of central economic and symbolic significance in West Africa for centuries. Control of the gold trade was the basis for a powerful kingdom which at one time dominated most of what is present-day Ghana: the Ashanti not only traded in gold but used it to make elaborate chiefly regalia, from rings to headbands and staves, as well as more ordinary jewellery. The golden stool was regarded as the soul of the Ashanti nation. Gold artefacts are found in museums in Ghana and around the world, but they are still in regular use in Ashanti life, and not just confined to chiefs and festivals. Even gold trading inspired the creation of beautiful objects. Elaborate bronze weights, crafted in the form of animals or symbols, were used to measure gold dust. They are still made for collectors today.

Gold remains central to the Ghanaian economy, although diamonds, manganese and bauxite are also mined. From a 15 per cent share of export earnings in the mid-1980s, gold now accounts for the largest proportion of Ghana's export earnings, at 40 per cent. This reflects an increase in production from 300,000 to 1,700,000 ounces between 1986 and 1995 which went hand-in-hand with the reorganisation of the sector as a result of adjustment measures and new legislation on concessions.

The largest producer is the Ashanti Goldfields Corporation (AGC), which has often been regarded as a great African success story: since its privatisation it has been largely managed by Ghanaians and was one of the first indigenous companies to be listed on international stock markets. But AGC is 32 per cent owned by the UK conglomerate Lonmin (formerly known as Lonrho), 20 per cent by the Ghana government, with most of the remainder controlled by international financial institutions (indicating that much of the profit is expatriated), and in 1999 fluctuations in the price of gold and gold derivatives left AGC open to take-over bids.

Large-scale gold extraction is highly mechanised, offering little employment. It has also been blamed for environmental degradation and contamination of drinking water in mining areas. Large companies are accused of riding roughshod over people's rights to land in the areas they explore and mine. Gold reserves have been exploited in the south of the country, but new finds in the north also have potential.

▲ *The 15th Asantehene, the late Otumfuo Nana Opoku Ware II, in full regalia. Otumfuo, a surveyor and barrister before becoming king, died in February 1999 at the age of 89. The new Asantehene, Otumfuo Osei Tutu II, was enstooled in April 1999.*

THE NEW GOLD RUSH IN THE NANGODI AREA

Gold rushes have historically caused all sorts of upheavals, and the Nangodi area in the Upper East Region is no exception. An area deep-mined for gold in the 1940s, the current gold rush focuses on the surface level. Young men from all over Ghana and West Africa have flooded in to make their fortune, and local women are also participating in the dig. Many of the Ghanaians coming to the area were made redundant under structural adjustment.

The rush has brought more money to the village economy. Those who sell produce and goods in the local market benefit, and there are opportunities for making money by providing services to the miners such as fetching water. But the rush also brings problems. Increased market prices affect local food security. The miners themselves face dangers as they dig pits without proper supports, and some of the mercury used in processing inevitably escapes into local water supplies. Miners have been accused of indiscriminately digging up land, even land under cultivation, without seeking permission, causing vast environmental damage as well as conflict. Other social problems are caused by the sudden influx of young men; on occasion, the army has had to be called in to maintain law and order.

▲ The miners dig pits and shafts between 2m and 15m in depth. The gold-bearing mud is washed, and mercury used to extract the gold and shape it into 'bush gold', which is then smelted over a makeshift furnace.

Ghana's diamond sector is smaller and has a history of corruption and struggling for survival. Production is mainly industrial grade. Adjustment ended the state's control over large-scale extraction but the private businesses now involved have not been able to restore production to even a quarter of 1970s levels. Ghana is also one of the world's largest manganese exporters; the potential for bauxite extraction is not fully realised.

Small-scale mineral extraction

Small-scale extraction of gold and diamonds are fast-growing mining sectors. Estimates state that a quarter of Ghana's diamond production is undertaken by individual miners.

Since small-scale gold mining was legalised in Ghana in 1989, many of those made redundant as a result of adjustment have looked to gold digging to make a living. The PAMSCAD programme has even assisted individual miners to improve the safety aspects of their work. Recently, small-scale gold extraction has started in the north of Ghana and is beginning to reverse the north–south trend in migration.

Manufacturing

The large-scale manufacturing sector in Ghana is relatively undeveloped; it includes textiles, drinks, food, plastics, vehicle assembly, and aluminium processing. Much of it is owned and

▼ *A wooden Akuaba doll. Traditionally believed to induce fertility in women, they are now produced for the tourist market.*

managed by the Lebanese community, but multinational companies such as Unilever and Valco also run factories. Various state-owned enterprises also used to be involved in manufacturing, so since liberalisation opened up the market to foreign competition in the 1980s, large numbers of factories have been closed, leading to huge job losses. In the future, taking part in the global economy will depend on Ghana's ability to provide an educated workforce.

Small-scale production and the importance of the informal sector

Production is dominated by small-scale producers, often operating in the 'informal' sector, which provides much more employment than formally regulated large-scale extraction and production. Small-scale manufacturing has grown as opportunities in the formal sector have reduced during structural adjustment. It is estimated that numbers in formal employment in the government and private sectors halved from 464,000 in 1985 to 230,000 in 1990. The small-scale informal sector now holds the key to survival of a large proportion of the population, especially women.

Problems in this sector include a chronic shortage of credit and lack of opportunities to receive training in new techniques, except through the apprenticeship system. Credit is rarely available in the formal banking system, and informal savings and loans organisations have little capital to offer. There is some government help: for instance, the National Board for Small-Scale Industries provides credit and wide-ranging training. NGOs such as the national Intermediate Technology Transfer Unit also offer assistance, but these services still cannot meet demand.

Traditionally, skills are acquired though family membership, fostering, or adoption into a skilled family or apprenticeship. Vocational education is also supposed to be provided in government institutions and in junior schools, but because they are short of equipment, students are unable to learn practical skills. With the increase in the size of this sector, there is a rising demand for vocational training, and the voluntary sector is trying to meet part of this demand.

One such voluntary organisation is the Ghana Young Artisans' Movement. It trains young people in vocational skills to enable them to start their own enterprises because formal-sector jobs are in such short supply. The project also aims to stem the drift of the youth to casual employment in the cities. Opportunities for vocational education in the north of Ghana are particularly poor. As the principal, Fatau Ibrahim says, 'The north is like a different continent in Ghana. There are many opportunities which don't come to the north'. Based in Tamale, the project seeks to redress this imbalance.

THE EXPERIENCE OF REDEPLOYMENT: MALEK'S STORY

Malek Benson has experienced the harsh effects of restructuring at first hand: at the age of 32, Malek is an apprentice wood carver in Foase village. Previously a worker with the Ministry of Agriculture, he was 'redeployed' during structural adjustment, an euphemism for redundancy. He received no compensation. Malek decided that he would acquire carver's skills in order to become self-employed: 'I prefer this job because you always get work to do. With government work, they can strike you off at any time.'

THE OPPORTUNITY TO LEARN A TRADE: YAHAYA'S STORY

Yahaya Alhassan is 22. His father has died and Yahaya helps look after his mother and his seven younger brothers and sisters. Yahaya used to hawk second-hand clothes, but he found that this work did not pay much and profits were irregular. 'I was only able to sell during the first week of the month, after workers had received their salaries.'

Yahaya now learns carpentry with the Ghana Young Artisans' Movement. A practical *and* theoretical education and tools are provided, unlike in a traditional apprenticeship, and fees are lower and spread over a period (the equivalent of US$40, payable in instalments over three years). The project also assists the young people to start their own businesses.

'When I finish the course I plan to set up my own workshop with the help of the Movement so I can provide for my family. I want to pass on my skills to my brothers. Only one of them has any education. I even dream of building a house one day.'

Valco, electricity, and the Akosombo dam

The Akosombo dam was built on the Volta River to produce hydro-electricity for Ghana. Cost considerations led the government to look for a commercial partner who would buy a large proportion of the electricity. An aluminium company was thought to be ideal, both because aluminium smelting requires large quantities of electricity and because it would make use of Ghana's bauxite deposits.

The USA, a major co-financier of the project, insisted that American companies were selected to build, own, and run the smelter – so Valco, owned by Kaiser, a US-based multi-national, got the contract. The Akosombo dam was completed in 1964.

Because of the flooding caused by the dam, 80,000 people had to be resettled. The authorities took a well-meaning welfarist approach, but villagers were dispossessed of their own land without measures being taken to acquire more for them elsewhere. New agricultural co-operatives and mechanisation schemes had been provided to replace traditional ownership patterns and methods, but they proved inappropriate and failed. New settlements had been built, but settlers were expected to move into half-built and unsuitable new homes with facilities that they could not sustain on lowered incomes.

Meanwhile, Valco had signed up to benefit from the cheapest electricity in the world, for 50 years and without being subject to normal taxation. The company's vast profits went to the USA, and the Ghanaian economy benefited little. Valco stated that due to the costs of developing the bauxite industry and transport infrastructure, it would import aluminium for ten years. Thirty-five years later, Valco is yet to source bauxite locally.

Recent underperformance of the hydro-electricity project due to low water levels in the Akosombo dam has led to power rationing in the cities but has had little impact on Valco. However, the Ghana government was able to renegotiate the contract with Valco in 1988, and it now pays a higher electricity charge.

Urban Ghana

About 36 per cent of Ghanaians live in urban areas, and this proportion is growing rapidly: estimates suggest that half of the total population will be urbanised by 2015. The largest city is Accra with a population of almost 2 million; other cities include Kumasi, Tamale, and Sekondi-Takoradi and Tema on the coast. Development seems to move at a faster pace in the cities: better infrastructure and telecommunications foster business growth and contribute to an atmosphere of opportunity and progress. As a result, migrants make up a significant proportion of urban populations. Most of them end up working in the informal sector and living in poor, overcrowded conditions or even on the streets. People may choose migration as a temporary or permanent strategy.

Nima

Nima is the largest and one of the oldest *zongo* areas of Accra. *Zongo* means 'camping place of a caravan' in Hausa, a language spoken mainly in northern Nigeria and Niger, but understood across West Africa. Most

BASHIRU AND AISHA

Bashiru El-Umar and Aisha Sambo met and married in Nima; they have one child, Hakeem. Bashiru is from northern Ghana; Aisha comes from Nigeria. Aisha sells aluminium cookware from home while Bashiru 'helps a friend' to supply government contracts. They have recently faced setbacks. Aisha sells her goods on credit and is owed a lot of money, so the business is at a standstill. Bashiru put his savings into a pyramid savings scheme which collapsed. They hope life will improve. As Bashiru says, 'God's time is the best'.

Bashiru and Aisha consider themselves lucky that they are able to rent two small rooms. They live in a typical compound house. There is no toilet, so you must queue at one of the five Nima toilet blocks. There is also no bath-room, so the tenants have constructed a makeshift cubicle in the street for bathing. Nima is so overcrowded that children are often sent to sleep in friends' rooms or in taxis or lorries (where they double as watchmen).

Educational facilities are reasonable in Nima, though: Hakeem attends a day nursery.

Nima is a noisy place, and people tend to be aggressive, but Bashiru and Aisha also like its vibrancy. Residents celebrate festivals from all the cultural traditions. Cinemas and football teams are popular. There are also strong self-help associations for men and women which maintain links with members who have migrated abroad.

▶ View of the main taxi park in Tamale, the main city of the Northern Region.

Nima inhabitants are 'northerners', Hausa-speaking Muslims from Ghana and from other West African countries. Working in the informal economy is the norm for most of Nima's residents.

Nima has been the largest 'slum' area of Accra. It is still overcrowded and lacks adequate sanitation, but there have been many improvements under a World Bank urban development programme. According to a recent survey, none of the poorest 10 per cent of Ghanaians live in Accra today. Still, people in cities may face unique problems unknown to most in rural areas, including social isolation: in times of crisis, they cannot depend on those around them for help.

▼ One of the fish markets at Elmina.

City markets and trading

Market trading in Ghana tends to be dominated by women. Women usually have little formal education, and this is a sector where the illiterate can participate. There is relatively little profit in market work, but women are trading out of

necessity. They carry the increased burden of providing for the family as costs of living are rising and husbands' contributions are declining because of low wages or unemployment.

Markets are taxed and serviced by local councils. In many areas, these services are poor, and there is no consultation on market organisation with market traders. From the traders' point of view, trading associations are of much greater importance.

Because sellers of one good in a market tend to operate together in one place and markets are cramped, customers must walk long distances in the market and often require porterage. In Accra and Kumasi, most portering is undertaken by *kaaya yo*. *Kaaya yo* tend to be migrant women from the north who move south on a temporary basis to earn money. They may do this work for a variety of reasons: women from some northern ethnic groups tend to become *kaaya yo* workers in the period after marriage before they have rooms built for them in their husbands' houses. These women often carry small children on their backs as they work with the aim of acquiring household utensils and clothes for married life. Others become *kaaya yo* because they have fled early or forced marriages or circumcision.

Kaaya yo tend to work and sleep in groups. They rent one room among themselves to sleep and store their belongings in. But they are vulnerable to exploitation and arbitrary persecution by the authorities. In Accra, *kaaya yo* earn an average of 80 cents a day.

Nana Akwa Akyanaa II, queenmother of cloth traders, retails and wholesales cloth in Kumasi Central Market, where women dominate in almost all areas of trade. There are strong women's market associations

KOJO'S STORY

Kojo Brenya shines shoes for a living in Accra and sleeps on the street at night. At the age of 15, illiterate and unable to speak English, he made the 350-mile trip from his home village to earn enough money to pay for an apprenticeship in tailoring and a sewing machine. He was unable to get money from his parents because they divorced, leaving his mother destitute and his father refusing to assist. Working every day from 6:30am to 5pm for three years, he has been able to buy the machine and earn almost enough money to start training. He has also been able to buy some clothes for his mother.

Kojo first came to Accra with a man who helps children to migrate. This man, who started out as a shoe-shiner himself, offers transport costs and a loan to get started at about 50 per cent interest. On first arriving in Accra, Kojo slept inside a classroom and paid the school watchman a small sum each week for this 'privilege'. To save this money, he moved onto the street after three months. As a new person ignorant of Accra ways, Kojo had his money stolen. Since then, he has saved successfully through an informal bank. On Sunday, the busiest day, he can earn up to US$3.

'GO SOMEWHERE ELSE'

If a place is not good for you
Go somewhere else
Ayé, ayé
If you don't find fortune here
Go somewhere else
In life you don't know where your luck lies
Even if you are rotting somewhere today
Some day things will improve
If you aren't happy here
Go somewhere else.

Noble Adu Kwasi, Highlife musician

headed by elected 'queenmothers'. The yam queenmother is the most senior. Nana Akwa Akyanaa II is the queenmother of the cloth traders: as well as settling disputes among them, Nana organises assistance for members in times of need, for example during illness.

Nana says that women dominate market trading in Kumasi out of necessity. Trading is something they can do to provide for the needs of their children which men do not cater for. 'Men cannot bear to sit from morning to evening and trade. Women are more forceful than men. Women must get up early and steel themselves to come to the market to get something to feed the children.'

Although some women are able to make huge profits, most are just getting by. In the cloth trade, as in many others, the main constraint is lack of access to capital. Most sellers cannot buy direct from the cloth factories, but must buy on credit from middlewomen. Inevitably this means that profits are lower for the retailers. An additional burden is inflation which makes it extremely difficult to try to save up capital to expand the business.

Clothing, festivals, and the visual arts

Abena Akyamaa, daughter of the queenmother of cloth traders in Kumasi central market, and some of her wares.

Ghanaians place great emphasis on elegant clothing, even in everyday life. This is reflected in spending patterns: large proportions of incomes are spent on dress. Most locally-made outfits fit perfectly because they are made-to-measure – by armies of well-trained seamstresses and tailors. Clients buy lengths of cloth in the market, often on extended credit. Cloth is valued according to its type and origin: bright cottons are popular; damask tie-dyed cloth and cloth printed using the wax method are valued over cottons printed in the ordinary and less long-lasting way. Even within these cloth types, a distinct pecking-order is discernible. For example, wax cloth made in Holland is generally prized above that made in England, which is in turn regarded more highly than wax cloth from Nigeria or Ghana. Prices reflect these valuations, and what you are able to afford reflects on your status. Cotton print designs are named and range from old favourites still in print to new patterns which reflect current events or express the allegiance of the wearer. Ghana's fortieth anniversary saw sales of a new 'Ghana 40 Years' design, and a pattern featuring giant mobile phones has recently become fashionable. During elections, designs are commissioned for political parties.

Clients take their cloth to the measuring session where they select the latest styles from the seamstress's album. This can become a lively discussion. Some styles are sewn in ways that make clever and economical use of the fabric, so that they can be unpicked and made into new fashions later on.

For everyday wear, most Ghanaians have to rely on second-hand clothes imported from Europe or north America, which are cheaper. In Akan, stalls selling these clothes are known as 'broni uawa' or 'dead white men'. In keeping with the Ghanaian insistence on neat and elegant dress, stallholders tend to wash, starch, and iron their wares so that they are presented to customers in pristine condition.

There are relatively few stores selling new off-the-peg clothes in Ghana. Locally-made ready-to-wear clothes – apart from children's school uniforms – are mostly couture. Ghana's designer fashion industry is thriving and renowned throughout West Africa, and primetime TV shows featuring the Accra catwalks make very popular viewing for men and women alike.

Occasion and traditional dress

The importance of everyday clothing is related to the central position that costume plays on occasions of religious or traditional importance. Then, dress is not only magnificent but has even more to say about the wealth and status of the wearer and the nature of the occasion.

Kente cloth is a traditional attire in Akan and Ewe communities. Woven in narrow strips about 10cm wide which are then sewn together,

▲ *Kente weaving is considered men's work. About 24 strips are needed to make a full-length cloth.*

▼ *The motif in this strip symbolises resistance against foreign military domination.*

dyes, colours, and designs vary from region to region but tend to be very striking. There are two rival claims about the origin of the cloth. One holds that kente comes from the Ewe village of Kpetoe and that its name derives from the Ewe words *ke* and *te*, 'open' and 'closed', referring to the back and forth movement of the shuttle on the weaver's loom. The other claim is that *kente* was first made in Bonwire in the Ashanti region.

Designs are named: they include *kyere tie* ('catch a leopard'), *fodua* ('Colubus monkey's tail'), and *adwense-asa* ('my skills are exhausted') in Akan. Some designs are reserved for particular individuals, such as the Ashanti king. *Kente* cloth has gained international appeal and has been used by top international fashion designers. Through the influence of pan-Africanism, it has also been used widely in the African American community in the US – some of whom trace their roots to the area that is now Ghana – for symbolic items such as graduation gowns. In Ghana, *kente* is worn at festivals and ceremonies.

In the north of Ghana, cotton cloth is also produced from narrow strips sewn together, predominantly in blue and white. This cloth is used to make smocks. While basic smocks are common everyday wear in the north as well as in youth culture in all the cities of Ghana, huge elaborately woven smocks, worn in layers, are the costume for northern chiefs on ritual and festive occasions.

Colours are very significant in occasion dress. For Akans, all those attending a funeral wear black and red, or plain black cloth. While women have fashionable styles sewn for them in these colours, men wear unsewn cloth in a toga style. At outdooring ceremonies for new-born children, Akans wear royal blue and white cloth.

The festival scene

Festivals are integral to the life of Ghanaian communities. They are occasions for prayer, music, dance, and song, for eating, drinking, and socialising, and even for making money. Festivals are always changing – just as they seem to replay the past they accommodate the new.

There is a huge variety of ancient festivals celebrating the traditional new year according to local calendars, celebrating the harvest, ensuring prosperity, renewing associations with the ancestors and deities, honouring chiefs, or commemorating past events.

The festival of Oguaa Fetu Afahye is the most important on the Fante calendar. It takes place annually on the first Saturday of September in Cape Coast (Oguaa). Asafo companies, the military units found in most Akan societies traditionally responsible for the defence of their town, dressed in full regalia, lead processions through the streets. It is an occasion for the Asafo and the people to renew pledges of loyalty to their chief.

The Kundum festival is celebrated by the Nzima and Ahanta on the west coast of Ghana. This celebration helps to renew the community through opening a space to expose social problems experienced during the year. Participants are allowed to ridicule their superiors and insult their neighbours. These 'victims' must listen to lengthy complaints against them without responding.

The Ga Homowo or 'hoot at hunger' festival in Greater Accra is held each year in August or September; it commemorates the hardships experienced during the Ga migration to the area some 600 years ago. The aim of the celebration is to mock the spectre of famine, in the hope that the humiliation will lead to a time of plenty.

▲ An entire month of preparations leads up to Afahye and culminates in bonfires, processions, speeches, and ritual ceremonies; one of the purposes is to secure a good season for Cape Coast fishermen.

▶ A procession during the Homowo harvest festival.

There are also 'modern' festivals, some of them associated with world religions, such as Christmas or Eid-Il-Fitr. Christmas in Akan is *buronya*, or 'the whiteman has got his festival'. Others are secular and of recent creation. National Farmers' Day, for example, is held on the first Friday in December; it is a national holiday, and prize-giving, celebrations, and dance are held in every district of Ghana. The biannual Pan-African Festival of Arts and Culture, PANAFEST, is held to promote the values of pan-Africanism as well as tourism.

Art

The art scene in Ghana is dynamic and varied. Art and craft makers were producing in their localities and for wealthier patrons, such as chiefs, well before formal education was widespread. The idioms through which they worked included the adinkra symbol system, and utilitarian and ritual objects formed the dominant media. The introduction of art education in the twentieth century has led to the birth of professional fine art. Fine artists have drawn on an array of traditional and Western influences, media, and techniques to express their individual ideas. But they have also been called upon to use their work for more overt political purposes: to celebrate aspects of local culture which had been downgraded under colonialism, and to create new national symbols which would promote national allegiance and unity among ethnic groups.

There are almost 100 adinkra symbols which refer to Akan proverbs. They continue to be cast as brass weights used to weigh gold dust, printed on cloth, incorporated in exterior house decoration, and carved on stools for domestic and ritual use. Tourism has led to new departures in the use of adinkra symbols, and they can be found on everything from t-shirts to earrings. Fine artists have also made use of them: El Anatsui, a Ghanaian sculptor, has used a fusion of Akan and other traditional symbolism to speak of the insecurity and disorientation of life in contemporary Africa.

Wooden akuaba dolls are another ancient art form which is continued. They were originally carried by women in the south of Ghana to promote their fertility. Also carved for the tourist market, they have inspired artists such as the ceramicist Kwame Amoah who has created a series of Akuaba pots.

Street art is a very accessible and popular art form. Commercially oriented, its patrons are local proprietors of barbershops, night clubs, commercial vehicles, chop-bars (local restaurants), and beer or wine bars. Billboards advertise the commercial activity through depicting hairstyles, women pounding a fufu dish from yams, or patrons drinking palm wine from calabashes, using bright acrylic paints.

▲ *A piece of fabric using traditional Adinkra symbols.*

▼ *A traditional pottery bowl from 1935.*

Culture, tradition, and change

Traditional political organisation

Chieftaincy is a strong institution in Ghana which takes a variety of forms. In many areas of Ghana, there are female as well as male chiefs but male chiefs are in the majority and there are no female paramount chiefs. Chieftaincy adapts to and shapes politics and culture in Ghana. Although chiefs still perform traditional roles at all levels, for example in settling disputes and in social organisation, they also contribute to public policy making. Paramount chiefs sit in Regional Houses of Chiefs and are represented in the National House of Chiefs which advises the government on chieftaincy, land, and other issues. A national debate is currently taking place on the appointment of women chiefs to these chambers.

Other groups used to have an alternative system of political organisation without secular political leaders. Under colonialism, chiefs were imposed on some of these societies to assist with British rule. Today, many of these groups argue that they are given low status and little development funding because they do not have paramount chiefs and are not represented in the Houses of Chiefs. They have begun to demand paramount chiefs of their own.

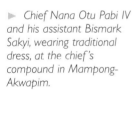

▶ *Chief Nana Otu Pabi IV and his assistant Bismark Sakyi, wearing traditional dress, at the chief's compound in Mampong-Akwapim.*

NANA KYAREWAA AMPONSEM II, ASHANTI CHIEF AND QUEENMOTHER

Nana Kyarewaa Amponsem II is an Ashanti 'queen-mother' of Kyerekrom, near Kumasi. The title *Nana* denotes a chief; it is inherited from grandmother to granddaughter through the female line. As well as being regarded as a chief, Nana is an official wife of the Ashanti king.

Because Nana is an Ashanti chief, she was installed into office on a stool. As tradition demands, her stool will be blackened on her death and placed in her sacred stool room with the stools of previous Kyerekrom queenmothers.

Nana shares her chiefly duties with her brother who is chief of the same town. 'He has a greater role in general town matters whereas my responsibilities lie with women's issues,' Nana explains. 'My duties have changed since my enstoolment in 1968. I still organise the women of her town and settle disputes between them, but I no longer officiate at girls' nubility rites which have died out in my area, partly because of the influence of the church. However, girls continue to come to me for advice. I have seen many new problems facing young women in Kyerekrom, including the rise in the abortion rate.'

'My status has also changed,' Nana continues. 'In the past, people would serve me but now people are too busy and treat me more like an ordinary person. At the same time, I am now consulted on matters of national policy affecting women. The First Lady of Ghana is a frequent visitor at queen-mothers' meetings where women's issues are discussed.'

Changing religion

Ghana is a very spiritual country. Belief in God is almost universal. Islamic, Christian, and traditional worship are all found but it is common for many people to practise an eclectic mix of religions in order to achieve pragmatic goals, and religious tolerance is the norm. In Langbensi in northern Ghana, for example, farmers join in Islamic prayers for a good harvest at the start of the season. But a prolonged drought can lead them to consult traditional rain-makers as well in an attempt to save their crops.

Celebrations of events like marriage or funerals often combine elements of world religions and local traditions. Within traditional religion, there is a belief in a supreme God but the world is considered to be populated with a complex array of lesser spirits. These spiritual cosmologies remain largely undocumented, are very dynamic, and vary between and within ethnic groups. Traditional religious practice focuses on those spirits who are regarded as close to mankind and believed to have an everyday influence on human affairs. Practice includes ancestor worship, personal shrine worship, and cults of shrines associated with nature spirits. In order to understand the actions and wishes of the spirit world, which may be manifest in misfortune or other events, diviners are consulted. Belief in occult powers such as witchcraft and evil medicine is also widespread throughout rural and urban areas.

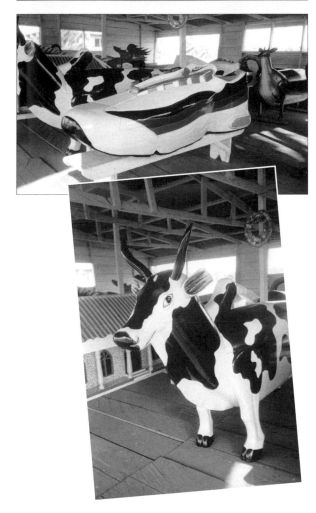

AKAN FUNERAL RITES

Akan funerals often incorporate a Christian ceremony but also follow traditional ideas about the long journey of the soul to the world of spirits (*asaman*). A funeral (*ayie*) attracts hundreds of mourners. Because of its spiritual significance, as many members as possible of the deceased person's lineage attend. Where hospital mortuaries are available, burial may not take place until several months after the person has died, to allow relatives to travel from abroad. These days, many families make videos of funerals so that those unable to attend can watch the proceedings later.

The body is usually laid in state on a Friday evening and a wake is kept. All mourners wear black and red cloth. As they arrive, they wail their grief, asking the dead person to convey personal messages to individual ancestors in the spirit world. The burial is performed on the next day. The dead person is given food and drink, and sacrifices are made to help them in the journey to the spirit world. Graveside prayers ask the dead person to prevent illness in the community, increase women's fertility, and ensure that the funeral expenses are recouped, expressing the dependence of the living on the ancestors. A church Thanksgiving service is held on Sunday.

After 40 days of mourning, relatives meet to perform further rites and to discuss inheritance matters. If the death is a chief's, this is the time when a successor is appointed. The final funeral celebrations are made one year after the death at the 'great funeral', which again attracts hundreds of participants.

Funerals are very costly, and all mourners are expected to make financial contributions before they leave. It is not unusual for relatives to make a profit in the end. Books are kept for future reference, and those in the community who do not contribute may not be helped if they have a death in the family at a later date.

▲ *A recent fad in Ghana: wealthy people can have any kind of coffin made — for example, a cow might be chosen for a cattle owner, an eagle for a chief, or even a fallopian tube for a gynaecologist. These unique coffins have also proven popular in the USA.*

► One of the oldest mosques in Ghana at Larabanga.

Islam

Islam is the longest established world religion in Ghana. Various sects are represented, including Tijaani (from Senegal), Ahmadiyya (from India), and al-Suna. There are Muslims all over Ghana, but Islam is concentrated in parts of northern Ghana and in the *zongo* areas of the big cities where northerners have settled. The national Chief Imam is recognised by the state as a spokesperson for the Islamic community.

In northern Ghana, many chiefs converted to Islam, and Muslims came to hold politically powerful positions within the traditional state structures. Early Muslim clerics brought writing skills and documented the early history of these states in Hausa, using Arabic script.

▼ Mustapha Ali, Tamale-based watch repairer and malam, uses a sand tray for divining purposes, along with a series of Islamic texts and a wooden board on which he writes with a special ink.

In recent times, Islamic organisations have also sponsored various development projects and schools. Primary schools teaching in English and Arabic are quite common in northern Ghana.

In cases of misfortune, people – whether they are Muslims or not – may resort to unorthodox Islamic practitioners, *malams*, for assistance. *Malams* use magical scripture-based and other techniques. Many people regard them as particularly potent in cases of sickness, so a person who normally practises traditional religion may resort to Islamic practice in the case of ill health. *Malams* are popular but do not pursue a high profile unlike their Christian counterparts.

Christian churches

Christianity became established in the south of Ghana in the 19th century. The church has developed relatively recently in the northern region where it has a lesser presence.

There is a great variety of denominations. The Roman Catholic and Protestant churches, known as 'orthodox' churches, are long-established and operate a wide range of development projects. Acting together as members of the Christian Council of Ghana and the Catholic Bishops' Conference respectively, the elite leadership form an important and often critical pressure group within Ghanaian politics.

In recent years, locally-founded spiritual, or miracle, churches have proliferated as people search for alternative solutions to problems in the tough economic climate. They believe that change is only possible through faith. Women form about 90 per cent of the congregations, perhaps because they bear the brunt of poverty. Hardships are often regarded as demons which must be cast out, and spiritual healing sessions are particularly popular. These churches are sometimes known as 'mushroom churches' because of the rate at which they multiply and because some of them are quite short-lived, set up by self-proclaimed prophets who wish to make a quick buck.

Other spiritual churches have become established as national organisations and also implement development projects. Rather than preaching the 'faith gospel' of other charismatic churches, they tend to emphasise the achievement of development through discipline and enterprise, like the Protestant churches. The Central Gospel Church, for example, is committed to educational development and is building the country's first private university. The close of Sunday morning service at its huge principal church sees thousands of worshippers, immaculately dressed in the latest Accra fashions, streaming out from the cool interior into the brightness and dust, fortified by sparkling gospel music and injunctions to work hard.

▼ An evangelical gathering in Kumasi central market. The reverend and his assistants use loudspeakers to reach their huge audience.

Changing kinship structures

All ethnic groups in Ghana share the concept of the clan or lineage, which includes all individuals who see themselves as descendants of a common ancestor. Descent can be traced through the male (patrilineal), female (matrilineal), or both lines. Clan leaders have traditionally looked after the

> Wisdom is like a baobab tree, a single person's hand cannot embrace it.
>
> *Ewe proverb*

well-being and spiritual welfare of the group. In clans with royal status, members are eligible to compete for chiefships held by the group.

In Ghana, there is a basic difference between the tradition of the Akan and the other ethnic groups. Most groups are patrilineal. In practice, this means that you belong to your father's clan, can compete for leadership within that clan, and inherit through the male line. But according to Akan ideology, a child gets blood from its mother whereas the contribution of the father is the child's spirit, *ntoro*. Because of this, an Akan person is considered to belong to and perform duties and responsibilities within their mother's clan (*obusua*) and can compete for leadership within that group. Traditionally, this has meant that a man's goods were not inherited by his own children, since they are in his wife's clan, but by his sister's children. There is evidence that inheritance is becoming more patrilineal over time, however. As social identity is now associated with education and employment as much as with clan membership, men wish to assist with the education and careers of their own children and make use of wills under modern legislation to ensure that they are inherited by their children.

▼ *Skills, values, and traditions are handed down through the generations.*

Violence and conflict in Ghana

At the everyday level, Ghana is a remarkably peaceful and crime-free society without significant ethnic or religious tensions. Accra is one of the few large cities in Africa where personal safety is assured in almost any area at any time of the day or night, for the resident and visitor alike. Ghana has often been sought as a haven by those fleeing conflict, and there is currently a large population of Liberian and Togolese refugees.

But there is some violence and conflict in Ghana, associated with ethnic differences, religion, land, politics, and gender.

The 1994–95 guinea fowl war in the Northern Region

A long history of intermittent ethnic tension and conflict in the north of the country culminated in the 1994 guinea fowl war, so-called because it was sparked off by a dispute in a market over the price of a fowl. Thousands of people were killed and at least 100,000 were made refugees as a result. Houses and crops were burned and looted, and schools, clinics, and wells destroyed. Peace-keeping and reconstruction cost the country dear.

Like many conflicts, the causes of the war were multiple. The fighting occurred between ethnic groups led by chiefs on the one hand and acephalous groups without secular leaders on the other. But at the root of the struggle was the region's underdevelopment and poverty. The acephalous groups perceived that the little development funding available was mainly targeted at the chiefly groups, and they were also convinced that their land rights were not recognised because they did not have chiefs. Apart from such feelings of resentment, there was also a religious dimension to the conflict. Many of the chiefly groups identify with, even if they do not practise, Islam, whereas Christian liberation theology has attracted many of the acephalous groups.

Peace initiatives

The Ghana armed forces are valued internationally for their contribution to both UN and West African peace-keeping initiatives and played an important role in restoring peace in the Northern Region during the guinea fowl war. Yet peace-keeping was not enough to reconcile the estranged communities and to rebuild co-operation for reconstruction and development. Government attempts at reconciliation met with little success.

A breakthrough came with the signing of a peace accord between the warring factions in 1996, which resulted from a process initiated by a consortium of local and international aid organisations working in northern Ghana. This consortium brought in non-government peace experts from Kenya, the Nairobi Peace Initiative, which worked with representatives of all the warring factions to reach an agreement. As part of this process, a new organisation, the Northern Region Youth and Development Association, was established. Made up of representatives from all the ethnic groups in the Northern Region, its aim is to solve ethnic disputes before they become violent and to achieve balanced development for the whole region. It has already diffused tensions in the region in many instances.

Other conflicts

Chieftaincy-related problems are not confined to northern Ghana. In the Ashanti kingdom alone, there are over 100 outstanding chieftaincy disputes. There have also been recent religion-based outbursts of violence, notably the conflicts between different Islamic sects in Kumasi.

Political violence relating to national government has been sporadic in Ghana. Although there have been many military coups, there has been relatively little accompanying violence. 1981 did see some violence, however, with several political murders and attacks on market women (who were allegedly overcharging consumers). In the early years of the PNDC regime, many political prisoners were taken. More recently, violence broke out during a protest against the government's planned introduction of VAT in 1995. Troops have also fired on student protests against government policy at the University of Ghana.

Violence against women

Violence against women in Ghana takes many forms. Wife-beating is a common and socially sanctioned form of violence against women in many areas, linked to women's lower social status in Ghanaian societies. Some women continue to see the practice as evidence of their partners' love.

Female genital mutilation is another form of institutionalised violence against women. It is practised for many reasons, but it is primarily a way of controlling women's sexuality and thus a form of oppression. Because of social pressures in its favour, surviving the process without flinching has been a source of pride for circumcised girls. However, social change has made it less shameful for girls not to be circumcised.

Female circumcision is practised in some northern Ghanaian societies, carried out by traditional practitioners using unsterilised instruments. Health effects range from short-term debilitation to long-term reproductive health problems and even death. Because it is officially illegal, female circumcision has gone underground. It is thought to be on the decline, but some cases still come to light if a girl has to be hospitalised.

Betrothal of girl babies, common in some rural areas, may be considered another form of gender violence. Since these girls must wed as soon as they come of age, their education is often ended prematurely.

Physical and psychological violence against women is also perpetrated in the continued incidence of witchcraft accusations, mainly aimed at older women and sometimes accompanied by violence. Here, women become the scapegoats for society's problems. Witchcraft accusations can also be interpreted as an attempt to limit women's economic successes and attached social prestige. Occasionally, men are also accused.

OUTCASTS' SETTLEMENTS

Outcasts' settlements provide a traditional 'solution' to the problem of violence against women accused of witchcraft. There are several 'witches' camps' in the rural areas of Ghana, under the protection of traditional authorities. Local beliefs state that witches can be cured; if cured, they may then be sent to these camps, largely for their own protection. If they went back to their villages, they would be subjected to violence.

In some cases, women prosper at these places. At Gambaga town, for example, the outcasts' quarters are next to a thriving market. Some of the women have been able to make money through this market and have become so successful that their husbands have come to join them from their villages.

Facing the future:
into the new millennium

▲ The mud-built men's rooms of a traditional compound contrast with the new central mosque being constructed in Tamale.

▲ If it is to prosper, Ghana must become less dependent on a single crop, and freedom and justice must become a reality with tangible benefits for the poor.

Where do the people of Ghana go from here?

For all the promises that structural adjustment will eventually bring a better life for all, only a few have benefited so far. With remarkable resilience, the majority of Ghanaians continue to bear the brunt of the austerity programme. Where service fees and high costs of farming inputs cannot be borne, health, education, and improved productivity must be forgone and so chances for a better life diminish. Sustained economic growth in the 1980s did little to improve the lives of the poor. Will current reduced economic growth work any differently?

To give adjustment any chance of success, a stable and accountable government is required. Ghana's historical record since independence shows that economic stress can easily produce political instability. In turn, political instability gives rise to yet further economic woes – a vicious circle. How far do the current economic problems present a risk to political stability?

In Ghanaian politics today there is more than a glimmer of hope. The transition to a stable, democratic, and accountable political process has been embarked upon. However, democracy is still in its infancy; authoritarian elements form part of the political process. Corruption has not been laid low, and there is still much work to do in empowering and educating ordinary Ghanaians about the democratic process and civil rights. For in the end, it is only if the electorate demand good governance and respect for human rights that politicians will be obliged to provide it. The work of the National Council for Civic Education, which has outreach staff in every district, is making a start in this direction.

Another cause for hope is the new Commission for Human Rights and Administrative Justice. It has been given free rein to investigate delays in the legal system and other human rights issues, including prison conditions and outcasts' settlements. Some of its proposals have been acted on by the government.

Democracy continues to develop, and the nation has put down yet more democratic roots: a new tier of local democracy was established in 1998 when elections were held for Unit Committees at the local community level. However, these do not yet have powers to raise revenues or allocate official budgets.

According to the new Constitution, Ghana's president may only hold office for two terms, so President Rawlings must step down in 2000. He has already named his successor, and his choice split the party for a time. All eyes are now on how the transition will take place. Yet a discussion of the details of Rawlings' succession would have seemed remarkable only ten years ago. At that time, the debate would have been about *whether* Rawlings and the PNDC would ever give up power, a familiar discussion about one-party states in the African context. The debate about *who* is to take over from Rawlings, then, is another positive sign for the future of democracy in Ghana.

There can be no development without peace at the local level. Local tensions, fights, and killings have done so much to retard progress in northern Ghana over the years, but there are more glimmers of hope for peace following the bloody conflict of 1994–95. Since they are local, local consensus and action is needed to end these conflicts. Following the war, community organisations have been set up for peace-building and development for the whole region, and these new forms of community action have had great success in quelling conflicts. Something good has come out of something bad. The foundation has been laid for further development in the Northern Region.

To address the local needs of ordinary Ghanaians, local planning is required, so the drive towards decentralisation in government departments is another positive sign. But at the moment it is far from achieving its goal: in all but a few cases, the influence of central government policy on the local situation remains strong. And huge development disparities continue, between the north and south, and between the urban and rural areas. There is a long way to go. Progress in setting up development projects which are planned in co-operation with local people is still largely confined to the non-government sector.

With growing peace, stability, democracy, and accountability, Ghana faces the future with hope. But the greatest fight is yet to be won: the everyday struggle against grinding poverty.

▼ *Ensuring that development reaches poorer areas will be one of the main challenges for the new government elected in 2000. Nima's inadequate sewerage system overflowed in 1995, leading to loss of life and destruction of property.*

Dates and events

c. 10,000 BC First archaeological evidence of human activity in Ghana.

c. 1298 AD Akan kingdom of Brong founded, other states arise.

1383 Arrival of first Europeans from France.

1472 Elmina castle constructed by Portuguese.

16th to 17th centuries Time of slave raids, wars, and important period of indigenous state formation.

1874 Gold Coast Colony established by Britain.

1878 Tetteh Quarshie introduces cocoa to Ghana.

1896 British-Ashanti war ends in exile of Ashanti king and establishment of Ashanti as a British Protectorate.

1900 First Africans appointed to the Gold Coast's Legislative Council.

1902 The British protectorate of the Northern Territories proclaimed.

1919 German Togoland becomes a League of Nations mandate under the Gold Coast.

1951 New constitution permits general elections; Nkrumah's Convention People's Party wins.

1956 Mandated Togoland unites with Gold Coast.

Legislature passes motion for independence; approved by Britain.

6 March 1957 Independence.

1 July 1960 Plebiscite creates a Republic: Nkrumah becomes President.

1966 Coup d'état brings National Liberation Council to power.

1969 Busia and his Progress Party win general election.

1972 Acheampong instigates coup, bringing the National Redemption Council to power.

1979 and 1981 Rawlings stages coups, Limann governs with a civilian administration in the interim.

1983 Severe drought and peak of economic crisis.

Beginning of structural adjustment, the stabilisation phase of the Economic Recovery Programme (ERP).

1985 National Commission for Democracy convened to plan for democratisation.

▲ *Independence Arch in Accra.*

1986 Second phase of ERP begins.

1988-9 New District Assembly elections.

1992 New democratic constitution. In May, political parties legalised. Rawlings wins presidential elections in November, and his party, the National Democratic Congress (NDC), succeeds in December parliamentary elections boycotted by the opposition.

1994-5 Northern conflict.

1996 General elections contested by all parties. Rawlings remains as President. NDC wins parliamentary election, but with a reduced majority.

1998 New Unit Committee elections.

1999 University of Ghana closed in the wake of violent student demonstrations against proposed fees increase. Campaigning begins for general elections in the year 2000.

◄ *European forts in Sekondi-Takoradi, from an eighteenth-century etching.*

Facts and figures

Area
238,537 sq km – roughly the size of the UK

Forest and woodland
37 per cent; annual estimated deforestation: 1.3 per cent

Population
18.3 million (1998 EIU estimate)

Average annual growth rate: 2.7 per cent (1990–97)

37 per cent of Ghanaians live in urban areas

Languages
Approximately 60, including Akan, Dagbani, Dangme, English (official), Ewe, Ga, Gonja, Hausa, Konkomba, Nzema

Currency
Cedis (C1=100 pesewas)
C3,400=US $1 (1999)

Education
School enrolment: 44 per cent (1995); 38 per cent of girls and 49 per cent of boys

Adult literacy: 65 per cent (1995); 53 per cent of women and 66 per cent of men

Life expectancy
57 for men, 61 for women (1996)

Infant mortality rate
74 per 1,000 live births (1997) – UK: 6 per 1,000 in 1997

Access to safe water
56 per cent (1995)

Access to health-care services
60 per cent (1995)

Gross National Product
US$6.6 billion (1997); US$370 per capita
Average annual growth (1988–98): 4.3 per cent

Shares of Gross Domestic Product
Agriculture: 38 per cent
Services: 37 per cent
Industry: 27 per cent
Manufacturing 9 per cent (World Bank figures 1998)

Inflation
74 per cent (1995); 19 per cent (1998).

Principal exports
Gold, cocoa, timber

Export earnings
US$ 2,004 million (1998)

Import spending
US$ 2,732 million (1998)

Communications
Telephone lines per 1,000: 4 (1996)
Television sets per 1,000: 16 (1995)
Radio sets per 1,000: 700 (1997 estimate)

Women
11 per cent of government ministers; 9 per cent of administrators and managers; 92 per cent adult economic participation (1995)

Labour force
61 per cent in agriculture; 29 per cent in services; 10 per cent in industry (1995)

Foreign debt
US$6,900 million (1998)

Aid
Total official aid: $654 million (1995)

Sources and further reading

History and culture

Kwame Anthony Appiah In My Father's House: Africa in the philosophy of culture (London: Methuen, 1992)

Arts http://www.marshall.edu/akanart

Francis Buah A History of Ghana (London: Macmillan, 1998)

Meyer Fortes The Dynamics of Clanship amongst the Tallensi (London: Oxford University Press, 1945)

Kojo Fosu Twentieth Century Art of Africa (Accra: Artists Alliance, 1993)

Esther Goody Parenthood and Social Reproduction (Cambridge University Press, 1982)

Jack Goody Technology, Tradition and the State in Africa (Cambridge University Press, 1980)

M. E. Kropp Dakubu (editor) The Languages of Ghana (London: Kegan Paul International, 1988)

Margaret Priestley West African Trade and Coast Society: a family study (Oxford University Press, 1969)

Peter Sarpong The Sacred stools of the Akan (Accra-Tema: Ghana Publishing Corp., 1971)

Enid Schildkrout People of the Zongo: the transformation of ethnic identities in Ghana (Cambridge University Press, 1978)

Martin Staniland The Lions of Dagbon (Cambridge University Press, 1975)

Economics and politics

LaVerle Berry Ghana: a country study (Washington DC: Federal Research Division, Library of Congress, 1995)

Lynne Brydon and Karen Legge Adjusting Society: the World Bank, the IMF and Ghana (London: Tauris, 1996)

Gracia Clark Onions are my husband: Survival and accumulation by West African Market Women (Chicago and London: The University of Chicago Press, 1994)

The Economist Intelligence Unit Ghana Reports

Paul Nugent Big Men, Small Boys and Politics in Ghana (London: Pinter, 1995)

Novels and tales

Ama Ata Aidoo No Sweetness Here and other stories (New York: Feminist Press at the City University of New York, 1995)

Peggy Appiah The pineapple child and other tales from Ashanti (London: Deutsch, 1990)

Ayi Kwei Armah The Beautyful Ones Are Not Yet Born (London: Heinemann, 1969)

Asare Konadu Ordained by the Oracle (London: Heinemann, 1969)

Kojo Laing Major Gentl and the Achimota Wars (London: Heinemann, 1992)

The environment

Kwamina Dickson A New Geography of Ghana (Harlow: Longman, 1988)

David Gledhill West African Trees (London: Longman, 1972)

Plunder in Ghana's rainforest for illegal profit (London: Friends of the Earth, 1992)

Current affairs and travel

Mylène Rémy Ghana Today (Paris: Les Editions de Jaguar, 1992)

Richard Trillo and Jim Hudgens West Africa the Rough Guide (London: Rough Guides 1995)

Godwin Yirenkyi Ghana In Brief (Accra: Institute for Scientific and Technological Information, CSIR, 1998)

Kwesi Yankah Woes of a Kwatriot: Reflections on the Ghanaian Situation (Accra: Woeli, 1990)

West Africa magazine (London: monthly)

Republic of Ghana website (with links to Ghanaian newspaper sites): http://www.ghana.com/republic/

Ghanaian radio stations website: http://ghanaclassifieds.com/Radio/index.html

Acknowledgements

The author would like to thank all the people who made this book possible in Ghana, particularly Ben Pugansoa and the staff and partners of Oxfam Tamale, Alhaji Abudulai, the chief and people of Bowku village, the Poku-Agyemang and Ali families, and Charles Afram.

Warm thanks also go Anke Lueddecke, Alice Iddi, and Charlotte Mongson, the staff at Oxfam's Gender and Learning Team, and the Naylor family for all their support.

Noaa bu puuhiri toori
(Mamprusi proverb. 'The chicken does not thank the mortar' – because it will always return to the mortar, where grain is pounded, to search for more).
Meda ase paa!
Rachel

The editor would like to thank Jonathan Ofori for his help in obtaining the photograph of the Big Six on p18.

Oxfam in Ghana

Oxfam GB has been working in Ghana since the early 1970s. There are currently 16 staff working for the Ghana programme, all Ghanaian nationals. Oxfam's work is limited to northern Ghana, the area of greatest need, and this is where the country office is located. Oxfam works in the sectors of health care, water, and income generation for women in isolated, rural areas where poverty is most severe. One of these areas, 'Overseas', is cut off by flooding during the rainy season. Other areas are characterised by chronic food insecurity.

Oxfam is also involved in providing vocational training in Tamale, in region-wide peace-building, and in research, networking, capacity-building, and advocacy on poverty issues at the regional and national levels.

Most of Oxfam's work is with local partner organisations which implement the projects. In the case of the 'Overseas' project, Oxfam runs the scheme directly.

Fair trade

Oxfam Fair Trade works with a large number of local producers all over Ghana through a partner organisation, Aid to Artisans Ghana. Oxfam Fair Trade buys and markets the goods in the UK, ranging from pots and baskets to brass ware and drums. Through selling Fair Trade chocolate in its shops and offering capacity-building advice, Oxfam supports the cocoa farmers' co-operative Kuapa Kokoo.

Index